北京胡同文化之旅

A CULTURE TOUR TO BEIJING HUTONG

李明德　编著
WRITTEN BY LI MINGDE

中国城市出版社

胡同老景尽收眼底
保存旧貌功不可没

舒乙

序

《北京胡同文化之旅》最早于 2005 年出版。这是一本介绍京城胡同文化的双语（中英文）书，受到了广大读者的欢迎。时隔十余年，此书又得到了出版的机会，这正是我国旅游事业蒸蒸日上的时代，北京的古老胡同传统文化和民俗更受到了中外旅游者和广大读者的重视与关注。

本次出版，文字和照片有所变化，尤其是近年北京市内已定为东城和西城两个区，以前的崇文区划归东城，宣武区划归西城。读者在阅读到原版胡同旅游专栏时，介绍的宣武区胡同游就是今天西城区胡同游的第二条路线，其景点并未变化。这里向读者说明，也是本次修订的一个重要原因。

另外，"老街巷风景线"中的著名景点增添了多幅照片，包括京城中轴线上的燕墩及永定门、名刹火神庙、法源寺、名将故地于谦祠、袁崇焕墓等多幅照片，以开阔旅游者的眼界。还增加了介绍北京流杯亭的文章及介绍 33 片文化保护区的文字。承蒙北京文史馆提供老北京四合院夏日风景（舒乙先生为本书写的序，此次考虑时间问题而撤下了），这里深表谢意！

李明德

2019 年 3 月

Preface

The book *A Culture Tour to Beijing Hutong* was published in 2005. It introduced the culture of Beijing's Hutong in Chinese-English, and met with a warm acceptance. It is going into its second edition. As it has a booming tourist industry in China today, more and more tourists pay more attention to the old traditional culture about Beijing's Hutong.

The second edition greatly improves on the first edition. For example, Chongwen District has been merged into Dongcheng District, and Xuanwu District has been merged into Xicheng District. So the Hutong tour route in Xuanwu District in the first edition is the second Hutong tour route in Xicheng District now. It is the important point in the second edition.

In addition, there increase some photos of spots in Scenic Spots along the Old Streets, including the photos of Yandun, Yongdingmen Gate, Huoshenmiao Temple, Fayuansi Temple, the ancestral temple, Yuanchonghuan Grave on the axis line. Besides, there are more contents about 33 batches of historical and cultural conservation zones in this book of the second edition.

Li Mingde

目 录

序 / 3

导言　胡同的起源与变迁 / 7

上篇　北京胡同的历史文化与建筑 / 11

　　一、北京四合院 / 12
　　二、漫话门楼建筑艺术 / 22
　　三、古老的门墩 / 32
　　四、有欣赏价值的门联 / 38
　　五、老街巷风景线 / 42
　　六、北京古戏楼 / 76
　　七、漫话北京奇石 / 86

下篇　北京胡同风情游经典线路 / 93

　　一、东城区胡同游 / 94
　　二、西城区胡同游（北线） / 118
　　三、西城区胡同游（南线） / 136

附　老北京胡同民情风俗画 / 156

　　北京的流杯亭 / 162

　　北京 33 片历史文化保护区 / 166

Contents

Preface / 4

Introduction The Origin and Change of Hutong / 7

Part A Historical Culture and Architecture of Beijing Hutong / 11

    I   Beijing Quadrangles / 17

    II Art of the Gate Architecture / 26

    III Piers for Ages / 36

    IV Valuable Couplets / 40

    V Scenic Spots along the Old Streets / 42

    VI Old Theatre Buildings / 77

    VII Peculiar Stones / 86

Part B Classical Travelling Routes to Beijing Hutong / 93

    I   Hutong Tour in East District / 95

    II Hutong Tour in West District (North Route) / 119

    III Hutong Tour in West District (South Route) / 137

Appendix

    Genre Painting of Beijing Hutong / 156

    Pavilions of Floating Cups in Beijing / 162

    The 33 Places under Historical and Cultural Protection in Beijing / 166

导 言　胡同的起源与变迁
Introduction　The Origin and Change of Hutong

　　北京是中国历史上的文化古城，也是世界文明史上一个壮丽的文化奇观。那古老的街巷是城市的脉络，由四合院比邻组成的街道，永远是正南正北、正东正西，恰似棋盘。人们称条条街道为"胡同"，至今已有700年以上的历史。元代自1267年至1276年（至元四年到至元十三年），建成了一座为今天北京市区奠定了基础的元大都城。元大都城城里的街道都有明确的规定：大街宽二十四步（约22米），小街宽十二步（约12米），胡同宽六步（约6米）。"胡同"这个词元代就有了。据专家考证，"胡同"二字源于蒙古语，意指"水井"，有水井的地方为居民聚集之地。另，元《经世大典》内有"火弄"一词，后来把"火弄"的平仄异读了。在元杂剧《单刀会》中有"杀出一条血胡同来"。由此可见，胡同在元代已成为习见之词。元大都有11个城门，胡同达400余条，如砖塔胡同、菜厂胡同、沙拉胡同等均是元代的街名，今天还是这样称呼它们的。

　　明灭元后，在元大都基础上重建了宫殿和街巷，又有了内外城之分。内城的主要建筑，南起正阳门，北至地安门，最北至钟鼓二楼，为中轴线。东西两边又形成与中轴线平行的南北大街。横向的胡同是在主干的基础上按规制建成。外城的街巷分布，也以中轴线为主干，前门大街为界，胡同贯穿其东西。此时的北京城分36坊，胡同增至1170条。

　　清朝建立后，定都北京，皇宫、城池、街巷沿袭明制，改称京师。街巷增扩，但总体布局无大的变化。内城胡同增至1477条，加上外城的600条，共计2077条。辛亥革命之后，北京城的胡同又有所增加，至新中国成立前，已增至3200条。新中国成立以后，北京的城市建设迅速发展，又有了新的居民区，至20世纪60年代，地图上所标示的胡同多达5000余条。

　　北京城胡同的命名是很有讲究的，也是一门独特的学问，其内容甚是丰富。有以典型建筑或遗址命名的，如黄寺大街，国子监街，东厂胡同，贡院头条、二条等胡同；有以历史上的名人命名的，如文丞相胡同、李阁老胡同、广宁伯胡同、石驸马大街、赵登禹路、张自忠路……也有以商业故地或商品名称来命名的，如灯市口大街，即因明代这里是灯市而留下此街名；烟袋斜街，是因清代至民国，直到新中国成立后，此处有多家卖烟袋的商店，街的形状又有些斜，很自然地定名为烟袋斜街了。花市上头条、下头条等胡同，也是因为此地曾卖鲜花和手工做的绢花、纸花而出名，后来留下了胡同名。

近些年来，随着城市现代化建设的深入，北京的高楼大厦越来越多，胡同在不断减少。为了使胡同这一北京古老、独特的建筑和民俗文化现象延续下去，政府将城区内有特色的胡同确定为历史文化保护地区，这对保护古都风貌起到了重要的作用。"胡同游"旅游项目，深受各界人士及海外游客的欢迎。

Beijing is an ancient cultural city in Chinese history and it is also a cultural miracle in world civilization. The old streets and lanes are just like the venation of a city. The streets are composed by quadrangles which are always standing at the north and facing the south. The whole design is exactly like a chessboard. People call the streets Hutong which has a history of over seven hundred years.Yuan Dynasty, from 1267 A.D. to 1276 A.D. (the 4th to the 22nd year of Zhiyuan times), spent eighteen years in constructing the Yuandadu City which is the basis of Beijing. It is during Yuan Dynasty that there is a clear regulation of streets inside the city. The regulation goes like this:twenty-four horse steps (C.22 meters) is a street, twelve horse steps (C.12 meters) is a lane while six horse steps (C.6 meters) is a Hutong. So, the word Hutong exists since Yuan Dynasty. According to the experts, Hutong comes from the language of Mongolia which means water well. Where there is a water well, there is the residence of people. In Yuanshi Doctrine, there is the word Huonong. Then it is said that Hutong is the wrong pronunciation of Huonong. In the Yuan poetic drama set to music Dandaohui, there is an expression such as dashing out a bloody Hutong,which proves that Hutong has been a popular recognition in Yuan Dynasty. There are eleven gates for Yuandadu, and more than four hundred Hutongs inside the city, including the Zhuanta Hutong, the Caichang Hutong and the Shala Hutong which remain their names since Yuan Dynasty.

When Yuan was replaced by Ming, palaces and streets were rebuilt on the basis of Yuandadu, and it comes to be divided into the inner city and outer city. South to the Zhengyang Gate, north to the Di'an Gate, the inner city has a central axis starting from the Drum & Bell

Tower to the north. Two main streets parallel to the axis were built at the east and the west. Hutongs were constructed from the main street according to the different sizes. The streets and lanes in the outer city were also built by the central axis. The Qianmen Street is the boundary of the inner city and outer city. Hutongs were constructed along the east-west direction. At this time, Bejing had thirty-six lanes while eleven hundred and seventy Hutongs.

When Qing Dynasty took the place of Ming, it chose Beijing to be the capital but changed the name to Jingshi with the same regulation of palaces and streets. There isn't a big change in the design of the whole city although the number of Hutongs increased. There were fourteen hundred and seventy—seven Hutongs in the inner city and six hundred in the outer city which accounts up to twenty hundred and seventy-seven. After the Revolution of 1911, the number of Hutongs had an increase. Till the building of PRC in 1949,there has been thirty-two hundred Hutongs in Beijing,and the city comstruction has experienced a rapid development.New residential areas show up here and there,and there were more than five thousand Hutongs on the map in the sixties of twenty century.

The naming of Hutong is also a profound knowledge. It can be named according to the famous architecture or the relics such as the Huangsi Street, Guozijian Street, Dongchang Hutong, the First Lane and Second Lane of Gongyuan Hutong. It can also be named by celebrities in history such as the Wenchengxiang Hutong, the Ligelao Hutong, the Guangningbo Hutong, the Shifuma Hutong, the Zhaodengyu Road and the Zhangzizhong Road. There are streets named by the commercial center or the name of special merchandise, such as the Dengshikou Street which was a lamp market in Ming Dynasty and Yandaixie Street which got the name because there were many stores selling tobacco pipes in this diagonal street. As for the Huashi Upper Lane and the Lower Lane were both named since there were many flower stores and paper flower stores.

With the development of modernization of the city in recent years, more and more skyscrapers take the place of Hutongs. In order to preserve the symbol of traditional Beijing culture and history, the municipal government has set off many preservation areas for cultural relics which has an important role in relics preservation. Hutong Tour, as a new rising tour item, has become more and more popular among the tourists around the world.

上篇 / 北京胡同的
历史文化与建筑

Part A　Historical Culture and
　　　　Architecture of Beijing Hutong

一、北京四合院

　　四合院是北京胡同中的独特建筑，大多数坐北朝南，由北房、东西厢房、南房加院墙围合而成。在兴建时，依据主人的财力和要求及工匠的技术，建造的宅院在规格上也有所变化，又有大四合院、小四合院、三合院之分。大四合院多为二进或三进，进门是外院，经垂花门进中院，再转向后院。北房又称正房，和垂花门建在中轴线上；东、西厢房对称；南房又称倒座房，位置与中轴线错开一些。院的门楼都建在东南角，其方位按八卦中的"巽"位安排。院的基地多数为东西短、南北长的纵长方形。封建社会里的大家族多为几世同堂，因此又要求上下有别、内外有别、主仆分明，往往是老辈住正房（即是北房），儿孙住东西厢房或后院，南屋为书房。院里种枣树、海棠或石榴树，夏季搭架栽种葡萄，安置鱼缸养金鱼，老北京的俚语"天棚、鱼缸、石榴树、先生、肥狗、胖丫头"，就生动地描述了过去四合院里富贵人家悠然自得的生活情景。为什么要种枣树、石榴树呢？不仅是因为花香四溢，更喜的是秋天硕果累累，正合了居住在这里的人们多子多孙、人财兴旺的意愿。也有居民在院内栽紫丁香的，取其"紫气东来"的祥瑞之意。

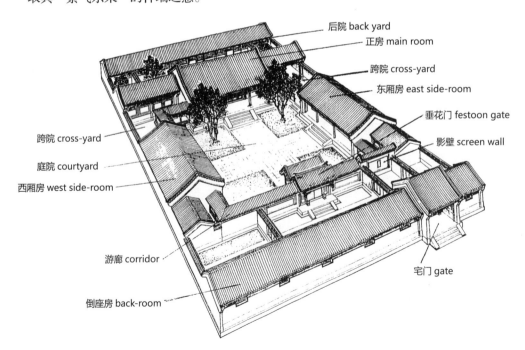

上篇　北京胡同的历史文化与建筑
Part A　Historical Culture and Architecture of Beijing Hutong

官宦之家的广亮大门
Guangliang gate of an official family

垂花门
Festoon gate

有着三百年历史的老式垂花门
（位于西城广宁伯街，已拆除。刘志宏 摄）
Old festoon gate over three hundred years (lies in Guangningbo street, dismantled. by Liu Zhihong)

垂花门，俗称二门（李海川 摄）
Festoon gate, or the 2nd gate (by Li Haichuan)

四合院建筑反映了老北京人的古老文化和民风。门楼的木门上用不同书法刻的门联，如"忠厚传家久 诗书继世长"等对句，展示了宅主人的品位或意愿。

走进院里，迎面是砖雕精细的影壁。清代王府、官宦之家门楼前多有墙砌的影壁，或称为影壁墙。在北京四合院的建筑中，影壁起着很重要的装饰作用。影壁分一字影壁和随墙影壁两种建筑形式，其造型分上、中、下三部分，顶部砌筒瓦屋檐，中间是磨砖对缝的影壁心，四角有雕刻的花纹图案，有的中间还雕有"平安""迪吉""福""吉祥"字样。下面是基座，加配青石砌成。其整体造型呈"一"字形的，人们称为一字影壁。这样的大影壁，在老胡同广亮大门的门楼对面还能见到，是四合院整体建筑的一部分。

夏季的四合院显得很是宁静，院中种植的石榴树、核桃树、枣树枝繁叶茂，花香四溢，随之呈现出硕果累累。人们在树荫下喝茶、下棋；晚饭过后，几代人相聚在一起谈笑风生，那更是独有情趣。农历五月初五是端阳节（俗称端午节），

夏季的四合院（马跃增 摄）
Quadrangles in summer (by Ma Yuezeng)

转角廊子
Corner-corridor

中院的正房
Main room in middle yard

西城区老四合院中木雕精美的垂花门
Festoon gate with fancy woodcarving in West District

中院的正房（刘志宏 摄）
Main room in middle yard (by Liu Zhihong)

庭院中的一角（刘志宏 摄）
Corner of courtyard (by Liu Zhihong)

对北京四合院中的人们来说，这是个很重要的节日。端午节据说是为了纪念战国时期大诗人屈原而立的节日，人们主要的吃食是粽子。相传，当年屈原投江之后，人们用粽子投入水中喂鱼，以免屈原的遗体被吃掉，这一习俗一直延续至今。老北京人过端午节，都要包江米、小枣粽子，或到糕点铺买粽子，院里还摆上夹竹桃、凤仙花、玉簪棒儿等鲜花，窗上贴红纸剪的蛇、蝎、蜘蛛、蜈蚣、蟾蜍的图案。小女孩在衣襟、辫梢上挂个用五彩丝线缠的小粽子，小男孩用雄黄酒在额头上写个"王"字。这些民俗是为了驱瘟避邪，尽管其中含有迷信色彩，但却反映了当时人们的良好愿望。

入伏以后，北京的天气越来越热，人们的饮食也随之有所变化。有段顺口溜儿："头伏饺子二伏面，三伏烙饼摊鸡蛋。"从饮食上看，由于天气热，面食做得多了，品种上也是简单省事为宜。除了西瓜上市，人们也增添了其他一些水果、凉食和饮料。老北京人还习惯把藕片、杏干、果肉等煮熟，放入冰箱一段时间之后取出食之，称此凉食为果子干儿。煮乌梅、冰糖，加些桂花，放凉后，便成了消暑解渴的酸梅汤；还有用鲜荷叶水与大米煮成的荷叶粥，均可称为盛夏的美食。

在这暑热季节，胡同里不时有叫卖声传到四合院里。清早有卖"生豆汁"的，紧接着又有吆喝"卖小金鱼儿""热云豆得了""新上市的菱角儿"的……大人小孩争着走出院门，选购自己喜欢的夏令食品。

今天，在众多的老胡同里，还保存着大量造型精美、环境优雅的砖木结构的四合院，其中有的还被列为市、区级文物保护单位。这些四合院大部分是民居，其间有几代人生活，保留着传统的老北京人的生活方式。有的院落里多户人家居住在一起，但大家相处得安祥和谐、团结友好。随着城市建设的飞跃发展，部分胡同的旧房进行拆迁改造，建成了楼房居民小区。对于已列入保护地区的胡同和有价值的院落，市政府正在尽力给以保留修缮，力求更好地展现北京老城区胡同和四合院的风貌。

Beijing Quadrangles

Quadrangle is a kind of special architecture type in Beijing Hutong. Most quadrangles, standing at the north end and facing the south, are compounds with the north house, the east and west side house and the south house around a courtyard. The size of a quadrangle depends on many factors including the economic capacity and specific demands of the owner, as well as the techniques of the architects, according to which the quadrangles are divided into big quadrangles, small quadrangles and Sanheyuan (triangle courtyard).Binary and temary quadranales are popular types among big quadrangles, which are composed of an outer yard by the gate, a middle yard through the festoon door and a back yard. The north house or the main house, together with the festoon door, lies exactly on the central axis,while the east and west side houses are required to be symmetrical, and the south one or the opposite house should be deflective from the axis. Its gate is usually at the southeast corner according to the Taoist thinking, the Eight Diagrams. The groundwork is like a rectangle, longer in south and north line and shorter in east and west. In feudalist society, it is popular that multi-generation lives together in a Kinship family, in which generation limit and grade difference is very strict.The elder generation lives in the main house, i.e. the north house, and the young generation lives in the side house or the back yard, and the south

转角廊
Corner-corridor

四合院内一角（刘松年 摄）
Corner of quadrangle (by Liu Songnian)

院中的屏门和带锦花窗的走廊（李海川 摄）
Screen gate in the courtyard and the corridor with Jinhua window (by Li Haichuan)

转角廊（李海川 摄）
Corner-corridor (by Li Haichuan)

老四合院中的花园
Corner of old quadrangle's garden

house is usually their study. There are Chinese jujubes, Chinese flowering crabapples and megranates in the courtyard and in summer grapes and golden fish can also be seen there. As the old Beijing slang goes, Sunshade, fish bowl, megranates; old Sir, fat dog, plumpgirl! It draws a vivid and idyllic picture of a well-to-do family in those old days. Why choosing the Chinese jujubes and megranates? The fragrance comes only to the second place, while in fact it is because of the rich fruits coming out in autumn to some extent, it reflects the traditional hope for offspring and wealth. For those who choose to plant lilacs, the favonian meaning weighs.

The traditional culture and folkway of old Beijingers can be seen through the architecture of quadrangles. We can take some examples to see how it is going. Couplets, for example, carved on the wooden door of the gate in various calligraphy, such as Honesty and tolerance will pass down son to son, while the Book of songs and the Four Books will spread generation by generation, show the taste or good wishes of the houseowner.

Stepping into the courtyard, you will find a screen wall with elaborate brick sculpture. The screen wall is built by brick during Qing Dynasty by the royal families and ranked officials and merchance prince. Yizi Screen and By-wall Screen are two main types of the screen wall. There is a upper part, middle part and lower part in one screen wall, the upper part of which is built as brick eaves, the middle part with polished bricks, and the lower part a pedestal built by bluestone. The middle part is carved flowers on the four corners,

院门外保存的一字照壁（李海川 摄）
Well-kept Yizi screen wall outside
(by Li Haichuan)

四合院里的影壁
Screen wall in front of the quadrangle gate

and there are always Chinese characters such as Ping'an (peace), Diji (enlightenment), Fu (fortune) and Jixiang (favonian) on. The screen wall in the Chinese character Yi (one) is named the Yizi Screen Wall. Today, the Yizi Screen Wall is still available to the opposite of the Guangliang gate in old Hutongs as part of the quadrangles.

Tranquility, there is nothing but tranquility in the quadrangles in the summer. Megranates, walnuts and jujubes are the most popular plants in the courtyards. They grow prosperously in the summer and take on a fruitful look in the coming autumn. People enjoy their free time here, drinking tea, playing Chinese chess or chatting after dinner. An important festival for those who live in the quadrangles is the Dragon Boat Festival which comes on 5th of the fifth lunar month in memory of the great poet Quyuan in Warring times. It is said that ancient people threw Zongzi into the river to prevent the body of Qu from being eaten by fish, after Qu committing suicide and then the tradition of eating Zongzi passes on. For old Beijingers, making Zongzi or buying Zongzi is a must in this festival. Besides, oleander, garden balsam and other flowers are usually placed in the yard, while decoupages, including snake, scorpion, spider, centipede and hoptoad in red are adhered on the glass-windows. Little girls

四合院门楼前的照壁
（张广太 摄）
Screen wall by the quadrangle gate (by Zhang Guangtai)

大四合院门前的照壁
（张广太 摄）
Screen wall in front of a large quadrangle (by Zhang Guangtai)

刻有砖雕图案及"戬毂"二字的影壁
Screen wall with brick-carved pattern and words of Jiangu

刻有花卉图案的影壁
Screen wall with flower pattern

雕刻"鸿禧"二字的影壁（李海川 摄）
Screen wall with the word of Hongxi (by Li Haichuan)

造型独特的雁翅影壁
Unique wild-goose-wing screen

are decorated with a multicolored mini-Zongzi either on the clothes or on the pigtails while little boys are marked a character meaning king on the foreheads. All the folk-customs are apotropaic-based, although superstitious, and they represent people's good wishes at that time.

Temperature roars up after the hot seasons, which change the diet of people. As the saying goes, Dumpling in the first Fu, noodle the second while battercake with egg for the third. Noodle acts as the main food in summer and watermelon as well as other fruit and cold drink also show up. For the senior citizens, they are used to have the lotus root, apricot and other flesh boiled and then freeze them in the refrigerator. This cold food is called Guozigan'er. Syrup of plum, which is made of ebony, candy and sweet-scented osmanthus, as well as lotus-leaf conjee, is delicious food in the hot summer.

In this season, vendors are active among the quadrangles. In the morning there is Soya-bean milk, then the little goldfish, new bean curd and fresh water chestflut. Adults, together with the kids, hurry to their favorites.

Today, the traditional brick-wood quadrangles can still be found in many old Hutongs. Since the courtyards distinguish themselves by elegant architecture and comfort environment, most of them are in the cultural relic list either of municipal or district-based. Civilian residence as they are, typical lives of old Beijingers are well kept there, with several generations living together, Some of the guadrangles are shared by several families who get on well with each other with the rapid development of city construction.

二、漫话门楼建筑艺术

在丰富悠久的北京历史文化中，街巷建筑占有重要地位。据史料记载，一些古老街巷形成于元代，经历明、清沿袭至今，大部分建筑及胡同名称均没什么大的变化。北京的王府大部分都是坐北朝南，分五间三启门王府和三间一启门王府，门前有石狮一对，左右各有上下马石和拴马桩。府门对面有砖雕照壁。朝阳门内大街路北的孚郡王府规模最大，至今保存完好。安定门内方家胡同路北的循郡王府，宣武门内大街路西、新文化街路北的克勤郡王府，整体建筑完美，近年又进行了修缮，保持了原貌。

官宦人家及富户的大四合院门楼，又分广亮大门和如意门两种。广亮大门门楼造型高大，门洞左右砖墙的上方戗檐雕有"富贵牡丹""狮子戏球"或"博古图"等精美砖雕。官宦之家的门洞屋檐下，左右均配木雕雀替一对，上面绘三朵云图案。部分门楼两侧还砌八字粉墙。如意门门楼造型很有特色，门楣与两侧砖角交接处砌成如意状的砖饰，表示"吉祥如意"；有这种砖砌图案的，人们称其为如意门。广亮大门和如意门在大门的上木框上，配有木制门簪，有的是四个，上面雕有字或花卉图案。如意门的门簪是两个，上面雕有"迪吉""平安"或"如意"等字。广亮大门及如意门

老四合院的如意门门楼（位于西城区孟端胡同路北，已拆除）
Ruyi gate of an ancient quadrangle (dismantled)

有八字粉墙的古老四合院门楼（张广太 摄）
Quadrangle gate with Fen wall (by Zhang Guangtai)

的木门上，均配有铁或铜制的响器门钹，往往是一对金属底盘上装树叶形或圆环形门钹。到宅院来的人，要拍门钹，音色响亮传至院内，主人听到就会前来开门。街巷中大多数四合院门楼为小如意门和随墙门。

　　街巷中四合院的门楼、门槛的造型装饰雕刻，有极高的研究价值，尤其在砖雕、石雕、木雕诸方面造型多样，内容丰富。从图案的内容看，多数是花卉、飞禽、走兽、人物故事……刻工们的技艺高超，展示了我国劳动人民的才华和智慧，虽然历经百年的自然风雨侵蚀，但今天依然显示出其光彩，为研究、考证北京街巷建筑史提供了宝贵的实物资料。在欣赏门楼雕刻艺术时，还应注意门槛两旁的石墩，建筑学术语称之"门枕石"。这些石墩造型多样，上面的石狮及图案雕刻，更是闪光的颗颗明珠。现存的门枕石主要分为两类：年代悠久的大都呈鼓形，正面看是卧状的狮子。传说，这样的狮子名叫"椒图"，是龙的第九子。另一种造型呈长方形，上雕卧式狮子。门枕石上石狮造型千姿百态，刻工精美；抱鼓石或方形石上的图案更是花样繁多，匠心独具。北京有句老话："有名的胡同三千九，无名的小巷赛牛毛。"如此众多的街巷，大部分的旧门楼门槛两侧配有门枕石，其数量很可观。在"文化大革命"破"四旧"中，这些门枕石上的石狮也遭了难。如今沿街巷考查，门前有一对完整石狮的门枕石已为数极少了。

保存一对上下马石的老门楼
Old gate with dismounting stones

老四合院的门楼（张广太 摄）
Gate of old quadrangles (by Zhang Guangtai)

北京胡同文化之旅
A CULTURE TOUR TO
BEIJING HUTONG

广亮大门门楼（刘志宏 摄）
Guangliang gate (by Liu Zhihong)

造型古朴的老如意门楼（刘志宏 摄）
Primitive Ruyi gate (by Liu Zhihong)

配有门簪和门墩的小四合院门楼
Mini gate with brims and piers

门头上有砖雕的门楼
Gate with top brick-carving

上篇　北京胡同的历史文化与建筑
Part A　Historical Culture and Architecture of Beijing Hutong

有八字粉墙的广亮大门门楼（位于东城区香铒胡同路北，已拆除）
Guangliang gate with Fen wall (dismantled)

造型独特的小如意门门楼
Unique mini Ruyi gate

如意门门楼
Ruyi gate

金柱门的四合院门楼（李海川 摄）
Quadrangle gate with golden columns (by Li Haichuan)

Art of the Gate Architecture

Streets and lanes play an important role in the long-living history of Beijing culture. According to the historical materials, many streets of Beijing came to being during the Yuan Dynasty. Although having experienced the Ming and Qing Dynasties, most architecture and their names remain the same. Prince Mansion of Beijing usually stands at the north and faces the south, including the five-to-one style and three-to-one style. A pair of stone lions are erected by the gate, and stepping- stones and horse-pegs are laid by the two sides. Opposite to the mansion gate, there is a brick screen wall. The largest mansion goes to the Fujun Mansion in the inner Chaoyang street. It is well-kept till now. Besides, Xunjun Mansion in the Fangjia Hutong in inner Anding Gate and Keqin Mansion in the inner Xuanwu Gate are all big mansioms and now have been restored to their origins.

Gates of royal families and the rich can be divided into Guangliang Gate and Ruyi Gate. Guangliang Gate is characterized by huge gate and brick brims of Bogu and lion-playing-ball. Wooden sparrow braces are set on the either side and Fen wall exist in some families. Ruyi Gate got its name for the special Ruyi-shaped brick-decoration at the crossing of the lintel and the two sides of the gate. This design means favonian and good wishes. Wooden brims are equipped on the frame of the Guangliang Gate and Ruyi Gate. It can be four or two with words or flowers carved on. There are usually two on the Ruyi Gate with benedictory words such as Happiness, Peace or Satisfaction on the brims. Iron or bronze cymbals are also equipped on the Guangliang Gate and Ruyi Gate. They are a pair of metal basis with a leaf-shaped ring or round ring. Visitors will beat the cymbals and then the master will come to the front gate hearing the ringingly sound of the cymbals. The commonest gate of quadrangles is little Ruyi Gate and By-wall Gate.

The decoration carvings of gates and principle columns in the residential house are of great value in research, especially for the various and meaningful brick carvings, stone carvings and wood carvings. The carvings focus on flowers, birds, beasts and folk stories. Sculptors' outstanding technique fully represents the intelligence and wisdom

图案精美独特的门头砖雕（马跃增 摄）
Special-designed top brick-carving (by Ma Yuezeng)

雕刻宝瓶图案的如意门门楼
Ruyi gate with vaselike pattern

门头砖雕近景（张广太 摄）
A close view at the brick-carving (by Zhang Guangtai)

如意门不同造型的门头（李海川 摄）
Various Ruyi top gate (by Li Haichuan)

古朴的《八骏图》门头砖雕（刘志宏 摄）
Simplicial Eight Horses picture carved on the top brick on the gate (by Liu Zhihong)

精美透雕人物与博古图的门头砖雕
Brick carving on the top gate with fancy character pictures

of the labor class. Although tested by hundreds of years, they are still shining today. All the preserved architecture and carving are invaluable in the research of Beijing street history.

The stone piers by the doorsill should also be paid attention to. They have various sculptures, such as the stone lion and picture carving which distinguish them a lot. The existing piers can be divided into two categories, one is long-living drum-shaped crouching lion, more like a mussel aside, which is said to be the ninth son of the Dragon. The other kind is like a rectangle with a crouching lion carving on the top. Almost every lion take on a different look, while the round mussels and the picture on the square stone also diversify to exhibit the extraordinary techniques of architecture. In order to see how many Hutongs there are in Beijing, we need to listen to the old expression, Hutongs named three thousand and nine hundred, numberless as the sand of the others. Since there are countless streets and lanes, and since almost all old gates in the street have piers, there should have been numerous piers as well. But the truth is it is hard to find a pair of complete stone lions, as most of them were destroyed in the Culture Revolution's so called Diminishing the Four Old.

有二百年历史的老门楼
Old gate more than two hundred years

造型优美的小如意门门楼（李海川 摄）
Mini Ruyi gate with fine sculpt (by Li Haichuan)

雕刻精美的如意门门楼
Exquisite carving Ruyi gate

上篇　北京胡同的历史文化与建筑
Part A　Historical Culture and Architecture of Beijing Hutong

清代府第的广亮大门门楼（张广太 摄）
Guangliang gate of Qing Mansion
(by Zhang Guangtai)

配有小型上马石的如意门（张广太 摄）
Ruyi gate with mini stepping-stones
(by Zhang Guangtai)

砖雕精美的如意门（张广太 摄）
Ruyi gate with nice brick-carving
(by Zhang Guangtai)

广亮大门前一对上下马石（张广太 摄）
Dismounting-stones by Guangliang gate
(by Zhang Guangtai)

北京胡同文化之旅
A CULTURE TOUR TO BEIJING HUTONG

雕刻"迪吉"二字的木门簪
Wooden brims with the Chinese characters Happiness and Fortune

保存下来的一对木雕门簪，图案是浮雕蝙蝠、佛手、石榴、桃子（原门楼已拆除，张广太 摄）
A pair of well-kept wooden brims with basso-relievo including the bat, Buddha hand, megranate and peach (the gate has been dismantled, by Zhang Guangtai)

雕刻"平安"二字的木门簪
Wooden brims with the Chinese characters Peace

铜制树叶形门钹一对（张广太 摄）
A pair of bronze leafshaped cymbals (by Zhang Guangtai)

雕刻"康宁"二字的木门簪
Wooden brims with the Chinese characters Health and Serenity

铁制圆环形门钹一对
A pair of iron round cymbals

上篇　北京胡同的历史文化与建筑
Part A　Historical Culture and Architecture of Beijing Hutong

竹林小鸟图案戗檐
Brim with birds in bamboo pattern

刻有太狮图案的戗檐（张广太 摄）
Brims with lion carving
(by Zhang Guangtai)

戗檐雕刻"鹿鹤同春"图案及下配富贵牡丹花篮
（张广太 摄）
Deer and crane pattern and the peony corbeil carved on the hip eaves (by Zhang Guangtai)

雕刻博古图案的戗檐（张广太 摄）
Brim with Bogu pattern
(by Zhang Guangtai)

透雕博古图案的戗檐
Hip eaves with Bogu pattern carved on

上图的局部
Details of brim

延年益寿图案的戗檐
（张广太 摄）
Brims with Longevity pattern
(by Zhang Guangtai)

为数极少的八仙故事图案的戗檐
（张广太 摄）
Rare brims with carving of the Eight Immortals (by Zhang Guangtai)

老门楼上戗檐的精美砖雕，这是三国故事，经受百年风雨，可谓珍品
Exquisite brick-carving on old gate brims, stories of the Three Kingomes

31

三、古老的门墩

　　四合院门楼木制街门的门槛两旁的石墩儿，建筑学上称为"门枕石"。这些石墩儿，俗称"门墩儿"。北京的民谣中有"小小子坐门墩儿，哭哭啼啼要媳妇儿，要媳妇做啥？点灯说话儿，吹灯做伴儿，明天早起给我梳小辫儿"的顺口溜。这是居住在四合院的儿童在大门前玩耍的写照，也说明了人们在孩童时代就与门墩联系在一起了。胡同中数以万计的门墩儿，其石雕造型不外乎两种，即呈鼓形和方形。年代久远的多为鼓形，近百年所雕多为长方形。其中造型设计绝大部分上面雕小狮子，下面的正、侧面雕有多种浮雕图案，其画面丰富多彩，真可谓是闪光的石雕精品。关于"门墩儿"上的卧式小狮子，是有讲究的。俗话说："龙生九子不成龙，各有所长。"这里的石狮是龙的一子，因它生性敏锐好闭，故专为主人守门，履行"随行闭门"的职责，这在清代《人海记》中"龙生九子"一节有论证。众多的抱鼓石上，石狮子的造型千姿百态，其刻工精美，受到了人们的喜爱。鼓形及方形石墩儿正面及侧面浮雕的图案更是花样繁多，匠心独具。门墩儿在大小规格尺寸上是有所区别的。王府与百姓之家差异就很大。正、侧面上的雕刻图案，刻工的精细程度上也有所不同。大部分浮雕图案

配有小狮子的抱鼓石近照（张广太 摄）
Close view of drum pier with lion on (by Zhang Guangtai)

雕有石狮子的抱鼓石
Drum pier with lion on

刻工精美的抱鼓石近照（李海川 摄）
Close view of exquisite drum pier (by Li Haichuan)

图案精美的抱鼓石（李海川 摄）
Exquisite square pier (by Li Haichuan)

是花卉，如梅花、菊花、兰草、竹子等我国的传统名花草以及石榴、蝙蝠、玉笛、葡萄、如意等图案。也有雕刻人物图案的，如有的抱鼓石正面及两侧面的石雕为古代乐舞人，其图案造型优美，舞蹈姿态生动，给人们以美的享受。还有"福在眼前（钱与前为谐音）"这幅石雕，画面上精雕蝙蝠与古钱的图案，表示了宅主人的意愿，其寓意为"福在眼前，财源滚滚"。以上叙述的这几种图案，今天在胡同中细心观察还是能见到的。我们在胡同中观赏、考查时，会发现保持着一对完整石狮子的已为数寥寥。有的四合院门前石墩儿仅存一个完整小狮子，或一对狮子均头尾不全，伤痕累累。今天我们在胡同里能看到的完整无损的小狮子门墩，可谓珍品了。

一对图案精美的老门墩（李海川 摄）
A pair of nice ancient piers (by Li Haichuan)

一对刻工精细的老抱鼓石（张广太 摄）
Exquisite drum piers (by Zhang Guangtai)

古老的造型奇特的抱鼓石门墩
Old drum pier in vagary pattern

古老抱鼓石近景（张广太 摄）
A close view at the old drum pier (by Zhang Guangtai)

造型优美的方门墩（张广太 摄）
Exquisite square pier (by Zhang Guangtai)

刻有不同图案的方门墩
Square pier with colorful carvings

北京胡同文化之旅
A CULTURE TOUR TO BEIJING HUTONG

保存一对老门墩的小门楼（李海川 摄）
Mini gate with a pair of old piers (by Li Haichuan)

雕刻精美石狮的方门墩
Square piers with exquisite lion-carving

方门墩局部近景
A close view of square pier

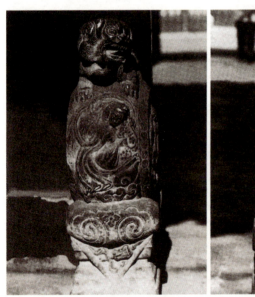 

西城一座清代王府门前雕有乐舞人图案的一对珍贵抱鼓石（张广太 摄）
A pair of highly-evaluated drum piers with the Dance in front of a mansion of Qing Dynasty in West District (by Zhang Guangtai)

雕刻精美石狮的方门墩（李海川 摄）
Square piers with exquisite lion-carving (by Li Haichuan)

保存一对方门墩的小门楼
Mini gate with well-kept square piers

古老的门墩
Old piers

雕刻花卉图案的老抱鼓石
Old drum pier with flower pattern

图案精美的抱鼓石
Exquisite drum pier

图案精美的抱鼓石(李海川 摄)
Exquisite drum pier (by Li Haichuan)

Piers for Ages

Stone piers are usually laid by the sills of the wooden doors of the quadrangles. In the balladry of Beijing, it says little boy sits on the pier, crying for a wife here, what's for? Chatting in the day and companying at night, Combing hair in the early morning. This balladry describes the kids who live in the quadrangle playing at the front day. It shows clearly that the pier has been connected closely to the childhood of many people.

There are two types of stone piers: one is those which look like a drum aside and the other is square one. The drum-shaped piers almost have a longer history while the square ones were carved within one hundred years. The design of piers doesn't vary a lot which all includes a little lion on the top with rich carving pictures on the front and the side face. There is a story of the crouching lion of the pier. It is said that the Dragon has nine sons and each is good at one skill. While, this son is acute and alert that enables him to be a good guard. The story can be found in *A See of Faces*, Qing Dynasty. It is tellable that so many lions were carved differently, but each is elegant and exquisite. As for the carving pictures on the pier, they all show originality in a unique style. The size of piers differs from the Prince Mansion to the commons. The design of pictures, as well as the manual work, differ a lot one to the other.

Most basso-relievo choose Chinese traditional well-known flowers, such as club,

一对完美石狮的方门墩（李海川 摄）
A pair of nice square piers with stone lions (by Li Haichuan)

chrysanthemum, orchid and bamboo, besides, popular drawing such as megranate, bat, flute, grape and Ruyi can also be found in the carving stone. Figure painting is another choice for the sculptors. The Dancer was carved vividly on the front and profile of the piers. The other basso-relievo is called Access to Happiness, and the bat and coin tell the good wishes of the house-owner, that is the happiness is of easy access and money will flow in.

The design above is visible today in Hutong with a careful eye. In our research of Hutong, it is really hard to find a pair of complete stone lions. In front of some quadrangles, you can see a complete lion standing alone or a handicapped pair, either having no head or having no tail. So, those complete ones are always highly evaluated.

老四合院门前一对抱鼓石
A pair of drum piers by old quadrangle

一对雕刻完美的抱鼓石
A pair of exquisite drum piers

雕刻太平花的方门墩
（张广太 摄）
Square pier with Peking mockorange pattern (by Zhang Guangtai)

雕有蝙蝠与铜钱图案的老方门墩
Old square pier with bat and coin pattern

不同图案的方门墩
（李海川 摄）
Various square piers (by Li Haichuan)

一对完美石狮的方门墩
A pair of nice square piers with stone lions

四、有欣赏价值的门联

四合院的门楼如意门最多，其中门上的对联至今也保存得最好，是胡同文化中的历史实物。在经受百年风雨的老木门上采用真、草、隶等不同书法雕刻，再上黑漆的门联，有着极高的欣赏价值，是书法艺术中的佳品。这些门联，有的反映出宅主人对传统文化的推崇和学识，如"忠厚传家久，诗书继世长"或"立德齐今古，藏书教子孙"。有三字或四字的门联，如"仁由义，德载福"或"国恩家庆，人寿年丰"，也有七字的门联，如"处世无奇但率真，传家有道为存厚"。有的门联反映了宅主人在历史上的功绩，如在清代文人纪晓岚故居的大门上，七字句的门联为"万卷编成群玉府，一生修到大罗天"，其意是颂扬纪晓岚编纂《四库全书》的功绩。也有表现宅主

保留着门联的门楼（李海川 摄）
Gate with ancient couplets (by Li Haichuan)

有门联和护铁的院门
Gate with couplets and iron rail

不同书法的门联（李海川 摄）
Sample couplet (by Li Haichuan)

人生活的时代的，如"物华民主日 人杰共和时"这副门联表达的是清末民初人们对民主共和的渴望。还有的门联既写出了风情，又与胡同的名称结合到一起，读起来很有学问，引起人们的深思。如地安门有条胡同称"白米斜街"，这里的一户人家，街门上的门联为"白雪远山图开大米，斜阳新柳春满天街"，对联写出了环境景观，并将"白米斜街"四字分藏在门联之中，给对联文化又增添了几分光彩。

Valuable Couplets

Ruyi gate is the most popular gate among Hutong, and then many valuable couplets are well kept as a witness of the change of Hutong culture. Formal script, cursive hand and official script handwriting was first carved by the gate and then painted by black lacquer. It is both of the enjoyment as well as the artistic value. The couplet is a way to show houseowners' canonization of traditional culture, and it exhibits the profound cultural insights of the family, such as Honesty and tolerance will pass down son to son, while the Book of Songs and the Four Books will spread generation by generation and Virtues distinguish at all the times, books direct to all the offspring. Three- or four-word couplets are also visible, Benevolence and righteousness, virtues and blessing or Kindness of a state and celebration of a family, longevity of people and abundance of year. Sometimes there are seven-word couplets, such as Ordinary but candid, patrimonyless but sainted. Couplet is also a good way to record the achievements of the house-owner. On the gate of the

篆字书法门联
Couplet in seal character

楷书书法门联（林访 摄）
Couplet in regular script (by Lin Fang)

蛮子门上的门联（李海川 摄）
Couplet on the Manzi gate (by Li Haichuan)

老院门上的门联（刘志宏 摄）
Couplet on the ancient gate (by Liu Zhihong)

famous scholar Ji Xiaolan, Qing Dynasty, in order to memorize his contribution in editing *the Imperial Collection of Four*, we can read such a couplet, Books pile up to the royal library, achievements roar up to the ninth Heaven. There are also some couplets used to describe the epoch spirits. Materials be abundant in democracy, individuals be outstanding with republic says an obvious yearn for the democracy in the late-Qing and early-Republic. Some couplets link the scenery and the name of Hutong together, bearing a deeper meaning for research. There is a Hutong called Baimixie Lane (White Rice Sidelong Lane). On one family's gate, we can see a couplet like Snow white on distant mountains looking to rice in the vicinity, setting sun with fresh willows adorning the street in spring. This is not only a description of the environment, but also it has the name of the Hutong hidden in, which adds more cultural odour.

五、老街巷风景线

  北京有着 3000 余年的建城史，是金、元、明、清的帝都。随着朝代的更替，古老的街巷留下了很多的历史、

  民俗遗迹，尤其在古建筑、寺庙、商业老街和店铺诸方面，依然保存着壮丽的景观和有研究价值的民俗文化遗物，这些景与物形成了老街巷的风景线。今天被列为保护地区的南锣鼓巷，有些老胡同还沿用几百年前的老名字；著名的清代园林——可园，至今保存完好，总督府旧宅院门楼前的一对上马石依然壮观；西城区砖塔胡同里的万松老人塔是目前京城唯一的一座元代砖塔；廊房头条和大栅栏地区的老店铺依然营业，欣欣向荣……这样的景观举不胜举。旧地重游会唤起读者对北京街巷历史和民俗文化的眷恋，各类遗存更是考查、研究京城文化的活化石。

Scenic Spots along the Old Streets

  Beijing, the capital of Jin, Yuan, Ming and Qing Dynasties, has a history of over three thousand years. Dynasty by dynasty, the old streets record many historical events while keeping many folk relics, especially in ancient buildings,temples, commercial streets and stores in the old time. The well-kept magnificent scenes and invaluable folk relics compose a special scenic line along the old streets. In Nanluogu Lane, which is listed as a preservation area, there are many old Hutongs which still remain their old names hundreds of years ago.Ke Garden,a famous Qing garden, is preserved well today. A pair of stepping stones in front of the old gubernatorial mansion always hold their pageantry. In Zhuanta Hutong in the West District, there is a Wansong Grandsire Pagoda which is the only completed brick pagoda of Yuan Dynasty in Beijing.Old stores in the 1st lane of Langfang and Dazhalan area are welcoming the customers everyday at present.Such scenic spots are countless in Hutongs. Revisiting a once familiar place with us will remind the reader of the history of Beijing Hutong as well as the folk culture. A good many relics is also a living fossil for the research of Beijing culture.

王府 Mansion

在北京的老街巷中，至今还保存着清代的王府。王府是按照《大清会典》的要求，分亲王、郡王的等级来营造的。朝内大街的孚王府是典型的五间三启门王府，安定门内方家胡同路北的循郡王府是三间一启门的王府。

There are some Mansion building of Qing Dynasty in old street of Beijing. The Mansion was constructed according to the Doctrine of Qing, including the social stratum of Qinwang, Junwang. Fu Mansion in inner Chao street is a typical Five-to-three gate Mansion, and Xunjun Mansion in Fangjia Hutong, inner Andingmen street is a Three-to-one gate Mansion.

保留上马石和栓马桩的老门楼
Old Gate with Stepping Stone and Picket Stake

在东城区飞龙桥胡同路北有一处200余年的四合院，其门楼的门框上配有四个木雕门簪，门楼左右有八字粉墙。大门正前方有上马石一对，左右各配石雕拴马桩，其造型是在雕成的石板上透雕圆形古钱图案，甚是古朴。门楼前有上马石的宅院多为官宦之家。清朝皇家规定：满洲贵族（王、贝勒以下）年未满60岁的都骑马往返，汉族官员准许乘轿。那时，京城内的满族官宦人家及富户子弟出门办事都要骑马，所以

三间一启门的王府（李明智 摄）
Three-to-one gate mansion (by Li Mingzhi)

五间三启门的王府（李海川 摄）
Five-to-three gate mansion (by Li Haichuan)

北京胡同文化之旅
A CULTURE TOUR TO
BEIJING HUTONG

门楼前设置大青石雕成的上马石和拴马桩。时至今天，京城一些老胡同里，大的宅院门楼还保存着上马石，可谓京城一景了。

There is an old quadrangle which is over two hundred years old in the north road of Feilongqiao Hutong in the East District. There are four wooden carving brims on the frame of the gate and a Fen-wall in Ba character on each side of the gate. There is a pair of stepping stones in front of the gate with a picket stake on each side. They are carved in the shape of ancient coin on the slate which are really nice and simplicial. Stepping stones usually appear in front of the gates of the official residences or the mansions of the merchant prince. It is strictly ruled that only the Manchu officials who are under the age 60 (and their ranks are lower than prince and Beile) are allowed to ride to-and-fro. While the Han officials are required to take the sedan chair. At that time, Manchu officials and merchants used to ride when they went out and that is why the stepping stones and picket stakes made in bluestone are visible in the front gate. Until now, the stepping stones are still visible in front of some gates of the old residences in Hutong, which can be called a special scene in Beijing.

保存着上马石和拴马桩的四合院门楼
Quadrangle gate with well-kept stepping stones and picket stake

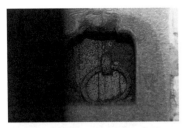

拴马桩近照，铁环为拴马所用（刘金城 摄）
A close view at the peg and iron-ring
(by Liu Jincheng)

拴马桩的另一种形式，石刻空的钱状孔
（张广太 摄）
Coin-shaped horse peg (by Zhang Guangtai)

有八字粉墙和上下马石的老四合院（原院已拆除，张广太 摄）
Old quadrangle with Fen-wall and stepping-stones (dismantled, by Zhang Guangtai)

京城最长的影壁 The Longest Screen Wall in Beijing

影壁又称为照壁，其位置在王府或四合院门楼的对面，可以让人们由院内走出大门时感到宽阔、整洁，以示里外有别。西城历代帝王庙前的照壁，可谓京城最长的照壁，有着近 400 年的历史，其规格也最大，总长 34 米，高 5.5 米，厚 1.3 米。

Screen wall, usually locates in the oppo-site of the royal mansion or quadrangle gate which serves as a division of the inner court and the outside and meanwhile, it makes people feel wide and clean when stepping outside. The screen wall in front of the Temple of the Ancient Monarchs in the West District might be the longest one since it is 34 meters in length, 5.5 meters in height and 1.3 meters in thickness which is over 400 years old.

铁影壁 The Iron Screen Wall

铁影壁是一块褐色岩石，正面刻狮子戏球图案，背面是麒麟苍松图案，雕刻古朴，苍劲有力，至今已有 700 多年的历史。元代，此影壁放在德胜门外土城附近。

20 世纪 90 年代初照壁前的情景
Old picture of the screen wall in 1990s

京城最长的照壁（位于历代帝王庙前）
The longest screen wall in Beijing in front of Beijing Temple of Ancient Monarchs

因其质地和颜色似铁，故民间称其为铁影壁，实为褐色火成岩，壁高 1.9 米，宽 3.6 米。后被移到德胜门内护国德胜庵前，至清代，这条老胡同就被定名为铁影壁胡同了。新中国成立前，曾有外国人想以重金买这块影壁，被该庵的僧人拒绝。为了能保住此文物，僧人将影壁左右上方的脊头毁掉了。1947 年，这块影壁又从此胡同移至京城北海公园里的澄观堂前。

The Iron Screen Wall is a brown rock over seven hundred years old. The picture of the lions playing ball is carved on the front while the kylin and old pine trees on the back side. The carving technique is quite praiseworthy. This wall was posited near the Tucheng outside Deshengmen in Yuan Dynasty and was named the Iron Screen Wall for its quality and color. In fact, the wall is a piece of brown igneous rock which is 1.9 meters in height and 3.6 meters in width. It was later removed to the front of the Desheng temple inside Deshengmen, for the reason of what the old Hutong was called the Iron Screen Wall Hutong. Before the foundation of PRC, a foreigner once showed interest in this iron screen wall and provided a quite attractive price, however was rejected by the shaman. In order to protect the historic cultural relic from being destroyed or bought, the shaman cut the ridge of the screen wall. Not until 1947, the screen wall was removed again from the Hutong to the Chengguan Hall inside the Beihai Park.

铁影壁
Iron screen wall

"金榜题名" 刻石 Carved Stone of Succeeding in a Government Examination

京城的老四合院里，至今还保存着科举时贺喜的刻石。这是一块高 80 厘米、宽 40 厘米、厚 35 厘米的清代以前的石物件，正面刻"金榜题名"的吉语，背面刻"玉虎"二字，历经二百余年，现刻石完好。

In the old quadrangle of Beijing, some carved stones are still kept which are used to congratulate the scholars who succeeded in the imperial examinations. This carved stone is from old time earlier than Qing dynasty. It is 80cm in height, 40cm in width and 30cm in thickness. On the front, there is a carving Jinbangtiming(succeeding in a government examination), while on the back there is Yuhu(Jade tiger) . It is a miracle that after the baptism of over 200 years, the stone is so well preserved.

"金榜题名"刻石正面
The front of the carved stone of succeeding in a government examination

"金榜题名"刻石背面
The back side of the carved stone of succeeding in a government examination

麒麟碑 Kyiln Stele

在东城区的麒麟碑胡同路北，曾有一座宽2米、高1.5米的元代石雕珍品，上刻古老的麒麟图案，其画面壮观独特，刻工技艺高超。几百年来，人们喜称它为"麒麟碑"。这件刻石被鼓楼文物所收藏，放在大厅正面，供中外旅游者观赏。

To the north of Kylin Stele Hutong in the East District, there was once a precious carved stone from Yuan Dynasty which is 2 meters in width and 1.5 meters in height. The fabulous animal Kylin is carved on the stone in extraordinary technique. It has been called for hundred of years. Now this stele is collected by the Drum-tower Institution of Cultural Relics and it is set in the main hall for view and admiration.

麒麟碑
Kylin stele

古老的过街楼（此楼已拆。韩树荣 摄）
Old crossing gate (dismantled, by Han Shurong)

观音院过街楼 Kwanyin Fane and the Arcade

在今天的菜市口大街，原有古刹观音院，分东、西两寺院，中间有一座过街楼相通。这是寺庙建筑的一种独特造型。过街楼的门洞上北面刻石雕"金绳"二字，南面刻"觉岸"二字，乃清道光年间所刻。过去，每逢进香之日，楼前香火极盛，门洞上贴满求福的字条，为京城一景。

There was a Kwanyin Fane once upon in Caishikou street. The fane was divided into the east part and the west, connected by an arcade which was a unique design among fanes. On the north side of the arcade, there was a Chinese character Jinsheng carving on it, while the south was Jue'an, which were carved in Daoguang year, Qing Dynasty. In those old days, there was a pretty busy sight here and blessing notes were stuck full of the gate wall.

当铺 Pawnshop

东直门内南小街的门楼胡同里有座当铺，其历史可追溯到宋代。当铺大门开在西边，门上有一碉堡状的砖砌方楼，甚是坚固，上设望孔六个。门框是青石的，设铁门。

京城仅存的百年老当铺
The only kept old pawnshop with one-hundred-year history in Beijing

旁院门上至今还嵌有石匾，上刻"泰和别馆"四字。此当铺为清代李氏所开，因其门上建方楼，似炮台，故附近居民称其为"炮台李"。这是今天老胡同里仅存的一家当铺。

There is a pawnshop in the Menlou Hutong in a small street, inner Dongzhi Gate. It can be traced back to the Song Dynasty. The gate is to the south and there is a solid tower like an emplacement on the top, with six guarding orifices. The doorframe is made of bluestone with an iron gate. On the stone plaque by the gate, there are four words, Taihebieguan. The owner of this pawnshop was a Mr. Li in Qing Dynasty, so the pawnshop was called Emplacement Li since it does like an emplacement. It is the only pawnshop that exists in Beijing Hutongs.

万松老人塔 Wansong Grandsire Pagoda

西城区的砖塔胡同因胡同中的一座砖塔而得名。此塔始建于金代，是座密檐八角九层的砖塔，完全为金元时的建筑风格。这座塔是为纪念万松秀禅师而建，所以俗称"万松老人塔"。

万松老人塔
Wansong Grandsire Pagoda

The Zhuanta Hutong in west District gets its name on the condition that there is a brick pagoda. The pagoda was built in Jin Dynasty. It is a Miyan style eight-square pagoda, nine floors in all which is a typical Jin architecture. This pagoda was built in memory of a Buddhist monk Wansongxiu and that is the reason why it was named so.

老店铺 Old Stores

在大栅栏商业区，至今还保留着清代的老店铺。这些砖木结构的二层小楼，建筑独具特色，楼下为商店，楼上是账房，也是店主人休息之所，当时多经营首饰、服装、鞋帽等。

店铺老房的一景（李海川 摄）
Two-storied shop in Dazhalan (by Li Haichuan)

大栅栏地区内的二层老店铺
Two-storied shop in Dazhalan street

In Dazhalan commercial area, there are still many old stores. Most of the stores have two floors, the ground-floor works as the store and the upper floor is the financial room and the resting place for the owner. The jewelry store, the toggery and the stores for shoes and caps take up a large percent of all the stores.

黔之会馆 Qianzhi Assembly Hall

这座中式老木楼位于宣武区的樱桃街61号，典雅古朴，气势恢宏，天井、廊檐环绕。此古建迄今已有二百余年，是清乾隆年间的黔之会馆，往昔考试的举子会聚于此。历史上的名人，包括清代乾隆年间大学士纪晓岚、民国时蔡锷将军都曾光临这里。

This hall is an old-fashioned wooden storied building, full of primitive simplicity. It is in the No.61 of Yingtao Street, Xuanwu District. Built during the Qianglong times, Qianzhi Assembly Hall has a history over two hundred years where ancient scholars as- sembled for exams. Many celebrities have once been here such as the Great Scholar Ji Xiaolan and the General Cai'e.

黔之会馆内景照(李明瑞 摄)
Qianzhi Assembly Hall (by Li Mingrui)

老冰窖
Old ice house

老冰窖 Old Ice House

今天,北海公园东门旁的雪池胡同和德胜门外的冰窖口胡同还保留着明清时代储存天然冰的冰窖。雪池胡同残存的黄琉璃瓦顶的老冰窖至今有着四百余年的历史,窖内建筑保存完好。昔日皇家夏季使用的冰,就是在冬天"拉冰"保存在这里。雪池胡同的冰窖,直至1979年才停止使用。

Ice house, which is used to preserve natural ice in Ming and Qing Dynasties, can still be found today in the Xuechi Hutong by the east gate of Beihai Park and the Bingjiao Hutong in outer Desheng Gate. The colored-glaze-roof ice house in Xuechi Hutong has an over four-hundred- year history. Even today, the inside of the ice house is well-kept. It is where the ice for royal usage from. It was not until 1979 that the ice house has been abandoned.

下马碑 Dismounting Stele

在东城区东华门附近和古老的国子监胡同里,今天仍完好保存着两座下马碑,碑

下马碑
Dismounting stele

位于东华门前的下马碑
Dismounting stele in front of Donghua gate

上刻着汉、满文"官员人等至此下马"。清代规定，凡骑马的官员从此经过，必须下马步行。

There are two complete dismounting steles in Beijing, one is near the Donghua Gate, East District, and the other is in the Guozijian Hutong. On the stele, dismounting here was carved in both Han and Manchu character. According to the Qing's royal rules, everyone, no matter how high the rank was, was demanded to dismount and step inside.

雁翅影壁 Wild-goose Wing Screen

这座巨大砖雕影壁在东城区一条老胡同里，是京城保存最完整的"雁翅影壁"。其造型呈"⁀\"形，砌工精细，磨砖对缝，在影壁墙上边角处均雕刻花草浮雕图案。整个影壁庄重美观，已有二百余年的历史。

The huge carven stone screen stands in an old Hutong in East District which is the bestkept wild-goose wing screen in Beijing. The figure of the screen is like the wing of a wildgoose. There is basso-relievo of flowers at each corner of the screen wall. The whole screen, older than two hundred years, looks pretty grand and majestic.

京城唯一的雁翅影壁（张广太 摄）
Wild-goose wing screen (by Zhang Guangtai)

泰山石敢当 Tai-Mountain Stone

京城的一些老胡同里，如果你细心观察，会发现有的四合院南房外墙壁上有或大或小的石刻，上刻"泰山石敢当"或"石敢当"等字样。此刻石为镇物。过去人们认为"泰山乃五岳之首"，其石可镇不祥。

If you have a close look at the outer wall of the south room in a quadrangle, you will find some stone inscription, big or small. Some write Corresponding to the Tai-Mountain Stone or Corresponding to That Stone. It is a sort of guard of the house. The older people believe that Tai-Mountain is the head of the Five Mountains, and the stone of Tai could guard the house from being intruded.

最窄的胡同 The Narrowest Hutong

前门外珠宝市街路西有条钱市胡同，可谓京城最窄的胡同了。这条小胡同总长不过50余米，宽度仅70厘米，只限一人行走，两人就得先后而行。这里还有几家住户，院内建有三层小楼，是清代的钱庄，至今保存完好。

The Qianshi Hutong in the west of Zhubaoshi Street, outside of the Front Gate, is the narrowest Hutong in Beijing. The total length of this Hutong is no more than fifty meters, and the width is only seventy centimeters which enable just one man walking through. Whenever two meet here, they have to pass in

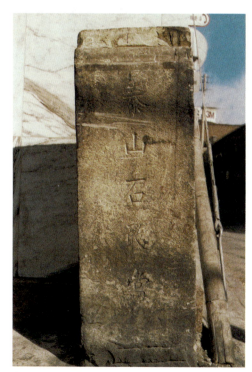

泰山石敢当石刻（李海川 摄）
Carving on Tai-mountain stone (by Li Haichuan)

turn. There are several families living here, and the three-storied building in the yard was a well-preserved ancient bank in Qing Dynasty.

黄瓦财神庙 The God of Wealth Temple

此庙甚小，仅大殿三间，特色是黄琉璃瓦，供奉财神。传说雍正皇帝未登基前曾路过此庙，对财神许愿，如能得皇位将重修此庙。后果然如愿，遂修缮此庙，换为黄瓦。该庙位于东城区鼓楼东大街路北。

The God of Wealth Temple lies in the north of Drum Tower street in Dongcheng District. The Temple is a small temple with only three rooms, marked characteristic with God of Wealth enshrined with the royal yellow tiles cover the roof. There is a vivid story. It is said that Emperor Yongzheng of Qing Dynasty had passed the temple, and promised that he would repaired the God of Wealth Temple if he enthroned. He got her wish later and kept his promise.

京城最窄的胡同——钱市胡同
Qianshi Hutong, the narrowest one in Beijing

广宁伯街老宅院
The Old Quadrangle in the Guangningbo Street

广宁伯街是西城区的明代老胡同。此四合院在路北位置，门楼及院内垂花门均为明末建筑，是座二进院落。人们传说这里即是明代广宁伯的宅第。该古建于 20 世纪 90 年代拆毁，今此处是金融街。

The Guangningbo Street is an old lane of Ming Dynasty in Xicheng District, and the Quadrangle with two-hall yard lies in the North of this street, and the entrance gate and inner festoon gate were built in late Ming Dynasty. It is said that the officer Guangn-

鼓楼东大街路北黄瓦财神庙（2008 年）
Temple of Wealth God(2008)

广宁伯街老宅院
Gate building of a Sihe Yard in Guangningbo Street

广宁伯街老宅院的夏天（马跃增 摄）
Old yard in the street of Guangningbo in summer(by Ma Yuezeng)

ingbo, Ming Dynasty, had lived here for many year. The old quadrangle have been destroyed 20 years ago.

涛贝勒府花园 The Garden in the Taobeile Mansion of Monarch

涛贝勒府位于西城区柳荫街 27 号。清宣统皇帝的叔叔载涛承袭贝勒，故称涛贝勒府。其花园部分花草茂繁，景色宜人，保存有清代的绣楼、长廊、亭台，是休闲游览的最佳去处。

Taobeile Mansion of Monarch lies in the No.27 Liuyin street in Xicheng district. Taobeile, the uncle of the last Emperor Xuantong of Qing Dyansty, lived in this Mansion of Monarch. The beautiful scenery in the garden is pleasure, and the buildings such as Xiulou,long corridor, pavilion of Qing.

袁崇焕墓 Yuan Chonghuan Tomb

袁崇焕是明朝末年著名军事家，爱国将领，官至兵部尚书。曾守卫辽东，抗击后

涛贝勒府花园
Garden in the Taobeile Mansion of Monarch

涛贝勒府花亭、假山
An artificial hill and an pavilion in it

袁崇焕墓（陈连生摄）
Yuan Chonghuan tomb(by Chen Liansheng)

袁崇焕祠（陈连生摄）
Yuan Chonghuan Ancestral Temple(by Chen Liansheng)

金，并取得京城保卫战的胜利。他的墓园在崇文区北京第五十九中学校园内，已修缮完好，并建有祠堂。现对外开放。

　　Yuan Chonghuan is a famous strategist, patriotic general of late Ming Dynasty. He had ever guarded in Liaodong Area(the Northeast of China), and won the war of the Capital agaist Houjin. His tomb is located in the No.59 Middle School, and be improved well now.

程砚秋故居 Cheng Yanqiu Former Residence

京剧四大名旦之一程砚秋先生的故居在西四北三条胡同。程砚秋先生是京剧程派唱腔的创始人，其代表剧目有《锁麟囊》《荒山泪》《英台抗婚》等，20 世纪 50 年代即被拍摄成舞台艺术片。此宅是个二进四合院，主屋保存了艺术家生前的戏装和剧照等珍贵资料。

Cheng Yanqiu is one of Four Major Dan Roles in China. IIis former residence lies in Xisi Bei Santiao Hutong(lane).He is the founder of Cheng style of Peking Opera, representative works such as Peking Opera Lock, Against Marriage. His former residence is two-yard quadrangle.

刘墉老宅 Liuyong Former Residence

此宅位于东城区礼士胡同 129 号，是清代乾隆年间大臣刘墉的宅第。这是个具有京城古建特色的四进大宅院，门楼高大，院墙砖雕精美，院内石兽和影壁、转角木廊很有特色，可谓四合院的精品。

Liuyong former residence lies in No.129 Lishi Hutong, Dongcheng District. It is famous officer Liuyong's former dwelling, a typical style of four-yard quadrangle with grand entrance gate. There are some elegant brick carvings on the wall, and characteristic kinds of stone sculpture of animals and screen walls and wood corner corridors.

灯市口教堂（东堂）Dengshikou Catholic Church

位于东城王府井大街 74 号，坐东朝西，是北京四大天主教堂之一，始建于清顺治二年（1645 年），本名圣若瑟堂，为葡萄牙人利类思和安文思二位神父创建。近年教堂进行修复，20 世纪 80 年代已恢复了正常的宗教活动。

Dengshikou Catholic Church, the East Church, is located facing-west in the east of Wangfujing Street, Dongcheng District. It is one of four cathedrals in Beijing. It was designed by two Portuguese priests in 1645, Qing Dynasty.

程砚秋故居
Gate of Cheng Yanqiu's former residence

程砚秋故居院内
The Inner Yard of Cheng Yanqiu's former residence

刘墉故居内景
Scence in the LiuYong's residence

刘墉老宅大门
Old gate of Liu Yong

西什库教堂（北堂）The Xishiku Catholic Church

西什库教堂位于西城区西什库大街 33 号，也称北堂。最初位于中南海西一个名叫蚕池的地方，始建于清康熙四十二年（1703 年）。光绪十二年（1866 年）移到西什库重建。哥特式建筑，高 16.5 米，钟楼塔尖高约 31 米，堂前左右各建中式黄琉璃

东城区灯市口老教堂（又称东堂）
East church in Dongcheng District

西什库教堂（王钊 摄）
Xishiku Catholic Church(by Wang Zhao)

瓦亭子，亭内是乾隆题字的石碑。一西一中，巧妙搭配，令人叫绝！

西什库教堂是天主教华北地区的主堂，教堂内的管风琴是北京最好的一座。

Xishiku Catholic Church, also North Church, is located in the No.33 Xishiku Street, Xicheng District. The Church was first built in Canchi, the west of Zhongnanhai Lake in 1703 during Emperor Kangxi, Qing Dynasty, and was removed into Xishiku area in 1866. Now it is a Gothic cathedral building, 16.5 meters high, with a 31-meter-high bell tower. In front of the entrance, there are two symmetrical pavilions which shelter a stone tablet with Emperor Qianlong's inscriptions, coverd with the royal-yellow-tiles roof of Chinese traditional style.

It is the main Catholic Church in the North China and there is the best pipe organ in Beijing.

炮局 Gun Bureau

位于东城区雍和宫附近的炮局胡同，清末是监狱。日本占领北京期间，爱国将领吉鸿昌就关押在此。新中国成立后，这里保留了清末民初的建筑。原围墙上的碉堡，至今还保存四座。

Gun Bureau lies in Paoju Hutong, Yonghe Lama Temple area of Dongcheng District. It was a jail in Qing Dynasty. Ji Hongchang , the famous anti-Japanese military officer has ever jailed here. After 1949, there still reserved the original appearance from late Qing Dynasty to early Republic of China (1912-1949), enclosing wall with four blockhouses.

现存监狱围墙碉堡一景
An old jail in Qing Dynasty

团城 Round City

团城紧临北海公园，始建于金大定年间（1163-1179年）。上建承光殿，为明代遗物，曾在清康熙年间修复。殿中佛像高1.6米，白玉雕成，堪称珍品。殿前有玉瓮亭，内放玉瓮重达3.5吨，是元代遗物，清乾隆十年（1745年）移至这里。

The Round City near Beihai Park is originally built in Jin Dynasty(1163-1179). In the Palace, Chengguang Palace, built in Ming Dynasty and rebuilt during Emperor Kangxi, Qing Dynasty.

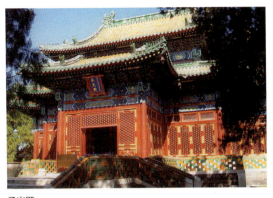
承光殿
Chengguang Palace

承光殿外景
Chengguang Palace in Beihai Park

there is a precious 1.6-meter-high jade Buddha statue; in front of the Palace, there is a pavilion with a jade liquor pot of Yuan Dynasty, transferred there in 1745.

鑫园客栈 The Xinyuan Inn

鑫园客栈位于烟袋斜街路北,是有着百年历史的鑫同浴池。大门口有对联:清泉淋浴精神爽,甘露润体气芬芳。浴室内有不同温度的水池,顾客在这儿洗澡还可以喝茶、搓澡、修脚。每天来这里的顾客很多。20世纪90年代初,这里改为旅馆,老浴池保持原貌,工作人员热情服务,获得了游客的一致好评。

The Xinyuan Inn lies in the north of Yandaixie Street with a history over one hundred years. It has been a reputation of several good common bath pools since last century. There is different water temperature in every bath pool here.

牛街清真寺 The Mosquein in the Niujie Street

该寺位于广安门内牛街。始为辽代阿拉伯学者纳苏鲁丁创建,是京城最大、历史最为悠久的清真寺。门前古老的牌楼甚是庄严,院内有望月楼,是伊斯兰教寺院中特有的建筑。礼拜殿坐西朝东,可同时容纳近千人做礼拜。礼拜殿后面是主殿,西侧是讲堂。寺内除古建筑外,还保存着清康熙年间"圣旨"牌匾,以及清道光年间的铜香炉。

老鑫园浴池
The Old Xinyuan Common Bath Pool

牛街清真寺
The Mosquein in the Niujie Street

The Mosque in the Niujie Street is located in the Niujie street of Guananmennei area, built in Liao Dynasty. Its designer is an Arab, NaSu Lu. It is the biggest mosque with the longest history in Beijing. The old Pailou(decorated archway) facing the entrance is majestic. There is an Islam style building named Wangyue(watching the moon)in the West, taking 2,000 worshippers. There is a well preserved tablet(The Emperor Kangxi wrote his will in Chinese calligraphy in Qing Dynasty). and a bronze burner made in the period of Ernperor Daoguang, Qing Dynasty.

天宁寺塔 Tianning Temple Pagoda

天宁寺塔位于西城区广安门北，始建于北魏孝文帝时期，这里原称光林寺。辽代在庙内建此十三层实心砖塔，通高57.8米，塔基双层，设有佛龛。上层雕有金刚力士像，威严精美。

The Tianning Temple Pagoda lies in the north oF Guanganmen, Xicheng District, built in Liao Dynasty. It is a thirteen storey pagoda made of bricks, about 57.8 meters high.

法源寺 Fayuan Temple

位于城南教子胡同。始建于唐贞观十九年（645年），是京城最古老的寺庙，有着千年以上的历史。门前有大石狮一对。山门对面建有宽大的影壁。院内有钟、鼓二楼，天王殿、大雄宝殿、观音阁等古建。毗卢殿堂前有巨大石钵，下有双层石座。石钵上雕刻有龙、麒麟、奔马，以及手持器物的人形、佛八宝、海水波浪，图案精美。此石钵至今保存完好，是珍贵文物。净业堂前廊两侧还有明代万历年间的童子拜观音、达摩始祖渡江图刻石，是佛教文化艺术珍品。

Fayuan Temple lies in the Jiaozi HIutong, in the south of Beijing city. It was built in 645, Tang Dynasty. lt is a temple with the longest history in Beijing. There are a pair of'stone lions in front of the entrance building of temple. A long screen waU was built on the opposite side of the temple. There are drum towers, bell towers, a Tianwang Mansion and a Daxiong Bao Mansion,and a Goddess Kuanyi Attic in the yard of temple. They are preserved well and open to the public today.

天宁寺塔
Tianning Temple Pagoda

法源寺
Fayuan Temple

法源寺大雄宝殿
The Great Hall of Fayuan Temple

万寿寺 Wanshou Temple(Longevity Temple)

万寿寺位于紫竹院西、长河北岸。始建于明代。山门坐北朝南。建筑分为三部分。中路是金刚殿、钟鼓楼、天王殿、大雄宝殿，后有假山和观音、文殊和普贤殿。尤其是后院墙中间的月亮门和左右各两个六角形透窗，墙与窗口上各有玲珑剔透的砖雕，可谓寺院中的珍品。该庙西院还建有行宫，因地处长河北岸，清代帝后前往颐和园是必经之路，帝后要到寺中礼佛拈香、休息，然后再登船启行。

Wanshou Temple (Longevity Temple) lies in the west of Zizhuyuan Garden Park, on the north bank of a long river, built in the Ming Dynasty. There are a Jingang mansion, bell towers, drum towers, a Tianwang mansion, a Daxionbao mansion, rockery, a Goddess Kuanyi mansion, a Goddess Puxian mansion, and a Goddess Wenshu mansion in the temple. It has been the Beijino Art Museum to exhibit artworks made in the Ming Dynasty and the Qing Dynasty.

万寿寺
Wanshou Temple

白云观 Baiyun Taoist Temple

位于西便门外的白云观，始建于元代，是北京最火的道观。院内有钟、鼓二楼，灵官殿，殿内奉祀王灵官，是道观镇守山门之神。后面建有玉皇殿、七真殿和邱祖殿（奉祀道长邱处机）。后院还有清康熙元年所建的四御殿。三清阁建筑很有特色，两层阁楼，楼上奉祀三清，也就是道教的三位尊神。后面还有元君殿和文昌阁以及花园假山等景观。每年春节这里还会举办庙会。

Baiyun Taoist Temple is near Xibian Men area in the south of Beijing city. There are bell towers, drum towers, a Lingguan mansion to commemorate a Taoist god named Wangling Guan. There are the Jade Emperor (the Supreme Deity of' Taoism) mansion, Qizhen mansion and Qiuzu mansion in the back of buildings above. There are the Siyu mansion and a two-storey attic called Sanqing which were built in the period of Emperor Kangxi, Qing Dynasty. 'Sanqing' is meaning of three Chinese Taoist gods. Besides these ones, there are rockery, a Yuanjun mansion and a Wenchang mansion in the back of those buildings. There is also a temple fair to be hold during the Spring festival holiday here every year.

白云观
Baiyun Taoist Temple

和敬公主府内十字廊全貌
Cross-shaped corridor in the Hejing Princess's residence

和敬公主府内十字廊 Hejing Princess Residence

位于东城区张自忠路 7 号。此府是清乾隆皇帝第三女和敬公主的宅第。现保存府门三间，门前大石狮一对。后有三进院落，各殿建筑均为清代风格。其中院建有十字廊子，正中是亭台，木结构建筑，样式独特，廊子分东西南北方向，与各屋相连接，既是古建中的一景，又为主人提供了方便，这在京城府第中独一无二。原十字廊建筑已于 20 世纪 90 年代拆除。

Hejing Princess Residence lies in the No.7, Zhang Zizhong Street. Hejing Princess is the third daughter of Emperor Qianlong, Qing Dynasty. A pair of stone lions stands in front of the entrance. There are three yards in the residence with the Qing Dynasty style. It has a good reputation of cross corridor made of wood material. The cross wooden corridor was pulled down in the 90s of 20 century.

意园 Yiyuan Yard

东城区麻线胡同 3 号原是清协办大学士敬澂宅第。其名"意园",大门坐北朝南,院内现有两株银杏树,花园内有太湖石及屏门,是圆明园遗物。石横额上刻有"春符"二字,两旁大青条石刻有"泉淙涧底琴音写,峰倚天边画景收",皆乾隆御笔。进石门后可看到假山及亭台。现此景观已异地移建到东四五条胡同。

Yiyuan Yard lies in No.3, Rongxian Hutong, Dongcheng district. It had been an officer JingHui's residence in Qing Dynasty. There are rockery from Taihu lake, relics from Chinese imperial garden Yuanmingyuan Garden, and two old ginkgo trees planted in the yard. It has a reputation of Chinese character " 春谷 (Chungu)" on the stone tablet written by Emperor Qianlong in Qing Dynasty in front of the rockery.

鲁迅博物馆 Luxun Museum

该馆位于北京阜成门内宫门口二条 19 号。著名文学家鲁迅先生自 1924 年即居住在这座四合院里,北屋是主人的居室及书房。屋前有两株枣树,为先生亲手所植。

The Luxun Museum lies in the Gongmenkou Ertiao Street, Fuchengmennei area, where the Chinese famous writer Luxu had lived since 1924. In the yard, two date trees was planted in front of living rooms by Luxun himself.

白塔寺(妙应寺)White Pagoda Temple (Miaoying Temple)

此塔位于京城阜成门内大街路路北白塔寺内。寺始建于辽代(1096 年),至今已有千年以上的历史;元代是妙应寺,是皇家宗教活动和百官习仪的场所。塔建于元代,高 51 米,属藏式喇嘛教佛塔,由著名尼泊尔工艺家阿哥尼主持建造,塔身洁白,甚是壮观,因此人们称这里为白塔寺。

The White Pagoda Temple (called the Miaoying Yemple also) lies in the north of Fuchengmennei Street, built in 1096, Liao Dynasty. There is also a 51 meters high White Pagoda built in Yuan Dynasty, designed by a Nepalese architect. There were many imperial religion activities to be hold every year in Qing Dynasty.

北京胡同文化之旅
A CULTURE TOUR TO
BEIJING HUTONG

意园内石屏门一景
Stone gate in the Yiyuan Garden

鲁迅故居一景（位于阜成门内）
Lu Xun's former residence

白塔寺
White Pagoda

京师图书馆遗址 Jingshi Library in Beijing City

清末京城第一家图书馆，始建于东城区方家胡同路北。该图书馆曾藏大量经、史、子、集图书，是京城的"书山""学海"。原"京师国书馆"大门于20世纪80年代被毁。

The Jingshi Library in Beijing City, the first one to the public in the late of Qing Dynasty, lies in the north of Fangjia Hutong. There ever were large numbers books of Confucian

京师图书馆
Gate building of Jingshi Library in Beijing

景德崇圣殿
Jingde Sage Mansion

classics, history, philosophy and literature preserved well in that time.

景德崇圣殿 Jingde Chongsheng Mansion

位于阜成门内大街的历代帝王庙，始建于明代，院内的景德崇圣殿是供奉历代皇帝和文臣武将牌位的地方。殿堂庄严宁静，很有气势。今已全面修缮，对外开放。

The Jingde Chongsheng Mansion lies in the Temple of Emperors of Imperial Dynasties, built in Ming Dynasty, and it was for enshrine and worship of Emperors of Imperial Dynasties. Today it is open to the public.

吕祖宫 The Lvzu Palace

此道观建于元代，位于元大都的西南角，今复兴门北街路东，是白云观的下院。其建筑分殿堂和楼阁，虽经数百年的风雨，但至今古建完整，是京城的一处景观。

The Taoist Lvzu Palace built in Yuan Dynasty, in the southwest of the relic of capital city of Yuan Dynasty (Yuandadu), now lies in the east of Fuxingmen north street. It's the lower yard of Baiyunguan.

吕祖宫外景（陈连生 摄）
Lvzu Palace (by Chen Liansheng)

吕祖宫院内一角
Inner of Lvzu Palace

如意门精美砖雕
Ruyi Gate of Family Suo Former residence

索家花园 The Family Suo Former Residence

这座花园位于交道门南秦老胡同35号，原为清代内务府总管索家老宅的花园部分，名"绮园"。院内有假山、亭、桥，还有一处仿江南园林的建筑——船形敞轩。其宅院如意门门楼砖雕图案丰富，刻工精美，至今保存完好。

The Family Suo Former Residence lies in No.35 Qinlao Hutong, Jiaodaokou area, Donocheng District. It has ever been the former residence of family Suo who was an overman of imperial palace in Qing Dynasty. It is also called Qiyuan. There are rockery, a stone bridge, a pavilion. Besides these, there is a building with the style of the south of

上篇　北京胡同的历史文化与建筑
Part A　Historical Culture and Architecture of Beijing Hutong

南新仓夜景（东直门内）
The night of Nanxincang (inner of Dong zhimen)

the Yangtze River, like a boat shape. The Ruyi gate building with the patterns of beautiful brick carving is preserved well today.

古粮仓 The Old Grain Bar

照片中的古粮仓为明代所建，位于东四十条 22 号。这高大宽阔的砖木建筑，用于贮粮，以备荒年赈济之需，至今还保存几座，已改为仓库，或文化演出场地。

The Old Grain Bar was built for grain storage in Ming Dynasty, lies in No.22 Dongsi Shitiao Street. The tall and spacious buildings are preserved and re-functioned as wardhouse and performing palace.

火神庙 The Huoshen Temple

该庙位于什刹海畔的火德真君庙，始建于元代，是京城最大的火神庙。院落三进，

73

今日火神庙（2008年）
Huoshen Temple(2008)

火神庙
Huoshen Temple

建有主殿、配殿和壮观的二层藏经楼。经过几百年的风雨，古庙早已破败，成了居民的大院。20世纪80年代，住户搬迁，文物部门对庙中的整体古建进行了全面的修缮，再现了火神庙的全貌，目前已对外开放，是鼓楼前的一大景观。

The Taoist Huoshen (Fire God) Temple in the Sichahai Lake area, built in Yuan Dynasty, was the largest Fire God Temple in Beijing. There are three courtyards including main mansion, wing building and grand attic mansion. The temple has damaged in recent year, and now has been reconstructed.

于谦祠 The Yuqian Temple

位于东城区西裱褙胡同路北（今新闻大厦东侧）。此老宅院原为明代英宗时兵部尚书于谦所居住，现大门上匾额为"于忠肃公祠"。院内设有展室。

The Yuqian Temple lies in the north of Xibiaobei Hutong. It has ever been the residence of Yuqian, an officer of Ming Dynasty.

燕墩 The Yandun

位于北京城中轴线最南端，始建于清乾隆年间，是一座高达十丈的方砖高台，上面有乾隆皇帝御制碑，碑面刻有"御制皇都篇"和"御制帝都篇"满汉文，至今

于谦祠
Yuqian Temple

燕墩（张泰昌 摄）
The Yandun（by Zhang Taichang）

永定门（张泰昌 摄）
Yongdingmen Gate Tower building（by Zhang Taichang）

保存完好。

The Yandun was built in the period of Emperor Qianlong, Qing Dynasty, which lies in the south of axle in Beijing. There is an article written by Emperor Qianlong.

永定门 Yongding Men Gate Tower Building

此城楼位于前门南，是中轴线上的重要建筑标志。始建于明嘉靖二十一年（1553年）。现为2004年在原址处重建。

Yongding Men Gate Tower Building lies in the south of Qianmen Gate Tower Building, built in 1553, Ming Dynasty. It is the important ancient architecture on the axle in Beijing city. It was reconstructed in 2004.

六、北京古戏楼

　　京城的戏楼有着悠久的历史。清代的皇家园林和各省在京所建的会馆,至今保留下来的古戏楼还为数不少。为什么要建这些戏楼呢?其历史要由二百余年前的徽班进京说起。1790年,清乾隆皇帝八旬大寿时,在京城举办庆典,南方久享盛名的徽班三庆、四喜、和春、春台来京献艺,戏剧史上称之为四大徽班进京。随后昆曲、秦腔的演员加入徽班演出,促成了京剧的形成和兴盛。在道光、咸丰年间,出现了第一代京剧演员程长庚、余三胜、张二奎等名老生。同治、光绪年间,京剧艺术有了更全面的发展,曾有一幅《同光十三绝》的国画,描绘了不同剧目和行当的名角。皇宫中的畅音阁戏楼、皇家园林颐和园中德和园大戏楼都在年节传艺人进宫当差,称为内廷供奉。京城里的一些王府中建有戏楼,王爷过生日也都召名角来宅子演出。恭王府花园中的戏楼,京剧艺术大家梅兰芳、程继先都曾来此献艺。在京各省的会馆也纷纷建了不同类型的戏楼;安徽会馆、平阳会馆、福建会馆内都有较大的戏楼,有时约演员演出,平时住在

正乙祠
Zhengyi Ci

这里的官员或赶考的举子们也会同台自娱自乐。北京城里保存着多座清代戏楼，在戏曲史上有着很大的影响。新中国成立以后，戏楼破旧，有的已做库房。20世纪80年代改革开放以来，故宫畅音阁戏楼、湖广会馆大戏楼、恭王府戏楼、正乙祠戏楼都进行了修复，经常上演传统京剧和曲艺，接待中外旅游者，古老的戏楼又焕发了青春。

Old Theatre Buildings

Theatre buildings in Beijing have a long history. There are many ancient theatres down from Qing imperial gardens and assembly halls of provincial officials. Why to build these theatres? It can be traced back to 200 years ago when Hui Opera first came to Beijing. In 1790, a celebration for Emperor Qianlong eighty-year-birthday was held in Beijing. A celebrated Hui Opera group Sanqing squad came to perform in the celebration, Then, Sanqing squad, Sixi squad, Hechun squad and Chuntai squad came afterwards and they together were honored as Four Hui Squad up to Beijing. Combined with Kunqu opera and Beijing opera, the Peking Opera comes into being and then flourishes. The first generation of opera celebrities turned up during Emperor Daoguang and Xianfeng times, Qing Dynasty, among which the most famous are the Laosheng Celebrities, including Cheng Changgeng, Yu Sansheng and Zhang Erkui. In Emperor Tongzhi and Guangxu times, Peking Opera bloomed to a brand new level. There is a painting Thirteen Excellence in Tongzhi and Guangxu Times describing different plays and characters in opera. Changyinge Theatre in the Forbidden City and Grand Theater in Dehe Garden in the summer palace, will summon opera players in on errand which is called inter court severs. Theatre is common in many royal mansions in Beijing and opera show will be on in the birthday celebration. Opera celebrity Mei Lanfang and Cheng Jixian had been on the stage in the theatre in Prince Yixin's garden. There are various theatres in each provincial assembly hall, among which the Anhui assembly hall, Pingyang assembly hall and Fujian assembly hall have bigger ones. Opera players sometimes will be invited to perform here which officials or candidates for imperial examinations who live here will amuse themselves from time to time. Qing's theatre building are the most common ones in Beijing which has effect on opera history.After the liberation, many ropey theatres have turned into warehouses. However, since the Open and Refrom in 1980s, Changyinge Theatre in Forbidden City, Grand Theate in Huguang Assembly Hall, theatre in Prince Yixin's mansion and Zhengyici theatre are restored to their origin. Now, traditional Peking Opera and plays are held termly to host the tourists from inside and outside China. The old theatres are blooming again.

德和园大戏楼 Grand Theatre in Dehe Garden

颐和园内德和园大戏楼，始建于1891年，戏楼高21米，台宽17米，分三层。戏台的顶板有天井，底层台板设地井。台板下有水井一口和四个水池，专为演出神话戏所用。根据剧情的需要，演员可由天井下降，也可以从地井钻出。有些剧目，如神话戏《金山寺》《水帘洞》《青石山》等，按剧情所需，配合布景，台上的众水族开打时，可利用台下的水井，使舞台上有泉水喷出，别开生面。在演出祝寿戏，如《万寿长春》《四海升平》《福寿延年》等时，台上角色众多，歌、舞并重，其场面更为壮观。据专家讲，当年一些大型祝寿戏，登台的角色多达200人。据记载，自光绪二十一年到三十四年，慈禧在这里共看戏262次，演出的多为京剧和昆曲。今天，德和园大戏楼已向游人开放。这里的殿堂中还展出清代宫中演戏时的戏装及部分道具。年轻的服务员身着清装，梳着"两把头"，足登"花盆底"鞋，在台上热情地为游客讲解。

Grand theatre in Dehe Garden in the Summer Palace was first built in 1891. It is twenty-one meters in height with three stories and seventeen meters in width of the stage. There is a patio in the roof and a patio underground. There is also a water well and four pools down there. When needed in legend playing, players can fly from the roof or jump from the patio underground. In the plays as Golden Mountain Temple, Waterfall Grotto and Greenstone Mountain, real water can burst from the well which makes the performance brilliant. Many players participate in the birthday celebration performance such as Longevity, Great Happiness around the World and Felicity which is a combination of singing and dancing. Some experts say that there have been more than two hundred people on stage once for

颐和园大戏楼
Grand theatre in Summer Palace

故宫畅音阁戏楼（张振光 摄）
Changyinge theatre in the Forbidden City
(by Zhang Zhenguang)

some big events. The Dowager Cixi has watched the play here for two hundred and sixty-two times, most of which are Peking opera and Kunqu opera. Today, the Grand Theatre is an open sightseeing place and tourists can have a look at the theatrical costume and property used in the performance. Young waitresses are dressed in typical Qing clothes, with a special makeup, to illustrate for the tourists.

畅音阁戏台 Changyinge Theatre

故宫畅音阁戏台台面宽阔，设计独具特色。台底下有井，可以及时汲水，按照剧情的需要，配以水彩。像《罗汉渡海》《地涌莲花》这样的大戏，都在此台上演出。《地涌莲花》戏中有四朵大莲花在台上出现，每朵花上坐着一尊菩萨，场面甚是壮观。这里台下的水井，除了供戏中用水所需，更重要的是起到聚音的作用，演员的唱、念及乐器伴奏都能获得极好的效果。

Changyinge Theatre locates inside the Forbidden City and it is also a huge theatre at that time. There are also well underground which enables water available in performance.

恭王府大戏楼内景
Grand theatre in mansion of prince Yixin

The famous plays such as Arhat Crossing the Sea and Lotus Welling-up were all performed here. In the Lotus Welling-up, four huge lotuses appeared on the stage with one Buddha in each lotus which was really impressive. The water well underground plays not only as a water supplier, but also a sound concentrated instrument which helps to get a better effect of the sound of the players and musical instruments.

恭王府戏楼 Theatre in the Mansion of Prince Yixin

在北京的柳荫街，有一座有着二百多年历史的府邸园林——恭王府花园。进入花园东路，就来到了著名的恭王府大戏楼。戏楼面积 685 平方米，建筑为三卷勾连搭全封闭式结构，楼内从墙到顶绘有盛开的藤萝与紫花图案，使人有在藤萝架下观戏之感。厅内摆设数十张紫檀木八仙桌和百余张太师椅，戏台高 1 米左右，约 8 米见方，为老戏台的凸出形。据介绍，当年王府里演戏时，主人与仆人同台，自唱自娱。

There is a more than two-hundred-year old mansion in the Liuyin Street in Beijing, the famous Mansion of Prince Yixin. The grand theatre, 685 square meters, shows up when entering the east road of the garden, which is a close Goulianda style architecture. Inside the building, liana and lucerne are carved from the wall up to the roof which makes you feel watching a play down the real liana. Ten rosewood old fashioned square tables for eight people and over a hundred fauteuils are placed in the hall. The stage is of old gibbous design, one meter in height and eight square meters in all. It is said that in those old days, both the master and the servants participated in the play as entertainment.

湖广会馆大戏楼正门（李思 摄）
The front gate of Huguang Assembly Hall (by Li Si)

湖广会馆戏楼 Theatre in Huguang Assembly Hall

该会馆在今宣武区虎坊桥路西，原为明丞相张居正故居。清嘉庆十二年（1807年）相国刘云房在此建湖广会馆。这里的戏楼是道光年间修建的，为木结构凸出形戏台，早年这里演出

湖广会馆戏楼全景
A panorama of the theatre, Huguang Assembly Hall

过京剧、昆曲以及地方戏。著名的京戏十三名伶之一的谭鑫培，就曾在此戏楼演出过。该戏楼与中国现代史有着密切的关系。我国伟大的革命先行者孙中山先生就曾多次莅临。今天，该戏楼已修饰一新，成为北京的戏曲博物馆。

Huguang Assembly Hall locates in the west road of Hufangqiao in Xuanwu District. It was once the residence of the Ming prime minister Zhang Juzheng and prime minister Liu Yunfang constructed the Assembly Hall on the basis of the old residence in the 12th year of Jiaqing Year in Qing Dynasty (1807A.D.). The theatre, with a protruding wooden stage, was built in Daoguang times where the Peking Opera, the Kunqu Opera and local opera had been performed. The famous one of the top thirteen actors, Mr. Tan Xinpei has performed on this stage. The theatre has a close relationship with Chinese modern history since the great revolutionist and leader Sun Yat-sen showed up here many times. Today, the theatre has been decorated into a brand new visage and is renamed the Beijing Opera Museum.

安徽会馆戏楼 Theatre in Anhui Assembly Hall

在北京宣武区后孙公园胡同路北的安徽会馆院内，建有上下两层的戏台一座，其台面宽阔，设有后台。两旁有包厢，显得很有气派。此处原是明末清初名人孙承泽的宅子，俗称"孙公园"。此戏台为宅主人宴客演戏而建。清代两部最有名的传奇——洪昇的《长生殿》、孔尚任的《桃花扇》都是在这个戏台上演出的。因此处是安徽会馆，黄梅戏的剧目进京，曾到此献艺。

Inside the Anhui Assembly hall, west road of Hufangqiao, Xuanwu District, there is a two-storied theatre. The stage of this theatre is pretty wide with a tiring-room at the back and balconies aside, which make it grand and lordly. This was originally the residence of a Qing celebrity, Sun Chengze, and it is the reason why it was named Sun Park. The theatre was built for the entertainment of the house-owner's guests. The two most famous plays, Palace of Eternal Youth by Hong Sheng and Peach blossom Fan by Kong Shangren, were performed on this stage. Since it was an Anhui assembly hall, Huangmei opera from Anhui province showed up on this stage too.

戏楼内的舞台（赵钢 摄）
The stage inside the theatre (by Zhao Gang)

安徽会馆戏楼外景（赵钢 摄）
Theatre in Anhui Assembly Hall (by Zhao Gang)

正乙祠戏楼 Theatre in Zhengyi Ancestral Temple

在前门西河沿，有座清代的银号会馆，其原址为古寺"正乙祠"。此院里坐南朝北有一古戏楼，其旁三面设有看楼环拱，形成四方天井。戏台不大，其名气却不小。一些老北京和京剧爱好者，提起此戏楼就会道出不少名人轶事。言派老生创始人言菊朋、名票陈墨香都曾在此演出。

Zhengyi Ancestral Temple, on the west bank of the Front Gate, was transformed into an assembly hall in Qing Dynasty. In the courtyard of the assembly hall, there is a theatre sitting at the south and facing the north. Round arch stands were built to three sides which thus constructed a square patio. Although not big in size, the theatre had a big fame. Opera celebrities such as the initiator Yan Jupeng of Laosheng in Yan Style and known Chen Moxiang have been on the stage both.

阳平会馆戏楼 Theatre in Yangping Assembly hall

在前门外小江胡同的阳平会馆里，现保存着一座建于清乾隆年间的老戏楼。该楼雄伟壮观，是一座十檩卷棚前后双步廊悬山顶建筑，戏楼内雕梁画栋，富丽堂皇。看台分二层，四角处设有木楼梯，戏台分上下三层，上有通口，下备坑道，可安置机关布景。戏楼两侧墙壁上绘有壁画。后壁嵌有石刻四块，记载平阳会馆的历史。

Inside the Yangping Assembly hall, Xiaojiang Hutong outer the Front Gate, there is an old theatre built in Qianlong times, Qing Dynasty. This theatre is a magnificent building with ten purline turn-up canopy and a Xuanshan roof. Inside the theatre, elegant carvings can be found everywhere, on the roof, the pillars as well as on the wall. The stand has two floors linked by wooden stairs at the corner, while the stage has a three-storied structure with an access on the top and a channel down set for the scenes of a performance. Frescos are visible on the side walls and four stone engravings are on the back wall.

东苑戏楼 Dongyuan Theatre

在北京的菖蒲河公园内，有一座新建的仿古戏楼，名为东苑戏楼。这里宫灯高悬，气氛典雅。舞台呈三面凸形，设二层楼，两侧有包厢。场内数十张八仙桌、木椅，可供200余人品茗观剧。

Dongyuan Theatre locates inside the Changpuhe Park which is actually a recentbuilt copy of ancient theatre. The theatre is decorated by traditional royal lights in an elegant atmosphere. Three-side protuberant stage the theatre has, it is a two-storied building with balconies at two sides. Tens of old fashioned square tables for eight people and manywood chairs are set down the audience which is available for over hundred people.

正乙祠戏楼大门
Gate of Zhengyi ancestral temple theatre

阳平会馆戏楼内景（吴赣生 摄）
Scene inside the Yangping Assembly Hall (by Wu Gansheng)

东苑戏楼
Dongyuan theatre

戏楼内一景
A scene of Dongyuan theatre

东苑戏楼外一角
Corner of Dongyuan theatre

七、漫话北京奇石

北京是金、元、明、清四朝的古都，有着许多优美的园林，大的是帝王宫苑，小的是私人名园。每游一山一景，都会听到传说和趣闻，从中受到教益。历经沧桑，现留存下来的大多为明、清两代建造的园林。这里，我们将名园中保留至今的奇石及其来历、传说介绍给读者。

Peculiar Stones

Beijing,the capital of Liao, Jin, Yuan, Ming and Qing Dynasties, has many beautiful gardens, the bigger ones of which are usually the palaces of the emperors, while the smaller private gardens. Every hill and scene is decorated with legend and anecdotes, both of which are instructive. Experiencing the aging process, nowaday gardens are mostly built in Ming and Qing Dynasties. In this book, we are going to present the peculiar stones including the history and legend.

佟府观音石 Kwanyin Stone in Tong Mansion

北京东城区灯市口大街的"佟府夹道"胡同内有座清代府第，原为康熙皇帝内亲佟国纲、佟国维的住所，至今已有二百余年历史。该府前照壁上镶嵌着一块巨大的汉白玉石。这块玉石上有青褐色花纹，每逢雨季，石面经水冲洗后，隐约可见山峦云雾之上，有一观音菩萨坐像，其发髻、披巾、眉眼均由天然花纹显现出来，坐像前有一香炉，烟雾缭绕，甚是逼真，可谓世间奇石。人们喜称这块美玉为"佟府观音石"。此府第现为北京166中学校址。

Tong Mansion passageway, lying in Dengshikou Street, East District of Beijing, is an old Hutong where there is a Qing mansion. The mansion was once the residence of Brother Tong Guogang and Tong Guowei, who are the relatives of the Emperor Kangxi. There is a

观音石
Kwanyin Stone

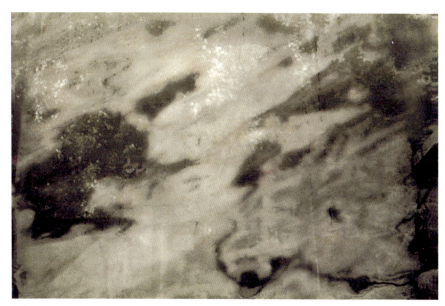
龙龟石壁
Dragon-turtle Screen Wall

huge white marble on the screen wall in front of the mansion. Cyan and brown lines are visible on the wall which turns up to be a Kwanyin sitting among clouds after rain. It is clear to see the bob, the amice, the vallas and the eyes which are all made up of natural lines on the stone. Thus, it was named Kwanyin Stone because of the vivid Kwanyin on the screen wall. Now, it is the location of Beijing No. 166 Middle School.

柏林寺内龙龟石壁 Dragon-turtle Screen Wall in Bolin Temple

建于元代至正七年（1347年）的戏楼胡同里，柏林寺的西院行宫内有石影壁一座。该石呈黑、褐、白三色，有天然的花纹，遇水即显现出龙龟腾飞画面，很是壮观，是块传世奇石。

The Bolin Temple in Xilou Hutong was built in the 7th of Zhizheng times, Yuan Dynasty(i.e. 1347AD). In the west yard of the Xanadu, there is a stone screen wall. It appears to be black, brown and white with natural lines on. Whenever there is water on it, the wall will change to be an incredible painting where there are a flying dragon and turtle.

北京胡同文化之旅
A CULTURE TOUR TO
BEIJING HUTONG

青莲朵
Qinglian Flower Stone

青莲朵 Qinglian Flower Stone

该石位于中山公园社稷坛西门外，造型独特，迤逦连接，纵横包络，嵌空玲珑，百窍通达。宋代此石在杭州的德寺宫内，明末画家蓝瑛曾为它作画。清乾隆皇帝南巡时，见此石后抚摩良久，赐名青莲朵，并记以诗。后遂辇送至京师，先存圆明园，后移至中山公园。

This stone is erected out the west gate of Altar of Grand and Grain, Zhongshan Park. It has a unique shape and lines on the stone appear to be exquisite and supernatural. It was first found in Desigong, Hangzhou in Song Dynasty. Lan Ying, a famous late-Ming artist has once drawn a picture on it. In Qing Dynasty, when Emperor Qianlong saw it during his south travel, he named it Qinglian Flower Stone and wrote a poem to praise it. Then it was sent to Beijing afterwards, to Yuanmingyuan first and then moved to Zhongshan Park.

独乐峰 Dulefeng Stone

在什刹海西岸恭王府花园内，耸立着一座直立的孤赏石，高达5米，绰约多姿，恰似屏障，可以见到"乐峰"二字，其"独"字却隐藏在此石的顶端。"独乐峰"取儒家"穷则独善其身"之义，同时也诉说了园主的心曲。

In the Mansion of Prince Yixin, west bank of Shichahai, there is an alone stone erecting. It is 5 meters in height which looks like a huge barrier. You can see the two characters Lefeng on the stone. The character Du was hidden on the top of the stone which is invisible from the front. The name comes from the Confucianism, depending on yourself and taking care of yourself when you are too poor to look after others. This is also the portrait of the owner's idea.

恭王府花园内名石独乐峰（李明德 摄）
Dulefeng in mansion of Prince Yixin (by Li Mingde)

颐和园乐寿堂院中名石青芝岫
Qingzhixiu stone in the Hall of Happingess and Longevity in the Summer Palace

天坛公园七星石
Seven-star stone in the Tiantan Park

青芝岫 Qingzhixiu Stone

颐和园乐寿堂前有块奇石名为"青芝岫",长8米,宽2米,高4米,颜色青润,形态独特,颇为壮观。此石原是明代赏石名家米万钟所采集。清代乾隆皇帝将其运至此处,题名"青芝岫",石上刻着众大臣的题咏。今巨石卧在雕刻着海涛云纹的石座上。

This stone locates in front of the Hall of Happiness and Longevity in the Summer Palace, which is 8 meters in length, 2 meters in width and 4 meters in height. The whole stone appears green and was collected by the Ming stone-collector Mi Wanzhong. Emperor Qianlong, Qing Dynasty, demanded this stone to be moved here and named it Qingzhixiu Stone with inscriptions of many ministers' on. Now, it is placed on a stone pedestal where surfy billows and clouds are carved.

七星石 The Rock of Seven-Star

天坛公园祈年殿东南空地处,有七块带有云朵花纹的大石。从整个布局的方位看,恰似北斗七星的阵式,人们称其为"七星石"。传说明代嘉靖皇帝来这里祭天,随行的道官对圣上进言曰:"空阔之地,虚造石填补,以保江山永固。"嘉靖皇帝大喜,后即安放了这组七星石。

四合院中的名石小玲珑
Little Linglong stone

Southeast to the Hall of Prayer for Good Harvest, the Temple of Heaven, there is a group of seven stones with natural cloud lines. The whole pattern is like Charles's Wain and it is how the name of the Rock of Seven-star comes from. It is said that Emperor Jiajing, Ming Dynasty, came to sacrifice the God of Heaven, a following Taoist said to the emperor that in order to consolidate the country, you'd better fill the empty place with substantial stones. Then, the group rock comes into being.

小玲珑 Little Linglong Stone

在东城区府学胡同一座老宅院里，保存着一块宋代奇石，高3米，呈桃状，名为"小玲珑"。该石生得小巧，空灵剔透，具备太湖石秀、瘦、皱、漏、透的五大特点。据考证，该石上"小玲珑"三个字雕刻位置极佳，是宋代名家所书。

This little stone is kept in an old house in Fuxue Hutong, East District. The Song stone, in the shape of a peach, is three meters in height and bears all the characteristics of Tai Lake stones that is elegant, lanky, crinkled, leaked and penetrated. It is said that the inscription on the stone was written by a celebrity of Song.

木变石 Wood Fossil Stone

故宫绛雪轩前有块独特的木化石，该石高1.3米，呈深褐黄色，树木的纹理清晰可辨。此石原为清代黑龙江将军福僧阿所采，后奉献给乾隆皇帝。

In front of the Jiangxuexuan, the Forbidden City, there is a peculiar wood fossil stone which is 1.3 meters in height. Dark yellow in color, the fossil has a clear line to recognize. It was collected by a Heilongjiang general, Fuseng'a, Qing Dynasty. Then the general paid it as an intribute to the Emperor Qianlong.

绛雪轩前的木变石（张振光 摄）
Wood fossil stone in front of the Jiangxuexuan
(by Zhang Zhenguang)

青云片 Qingyunpian Stone

在中山公园的来今雨轩东南角附近，有块特大的青石，上面刻有"青云片"三字，是清乾隆皇帝所题。该石四周还刻有赞诗八首。此石玲珑奇秀，高3米，长3.5米，是明代米万钟的遗物，后移至圆明园的时赏斋，再后移至此。"青云片"与颐和园内的"青芝岫"有雌雄石之美称：青芝岫为雄石，青云片为雌石。

Southeast to the Jinyulaixuan, Zhongshan Park, there is a huge green stone with Qianlong's inscription Qingyunpian on it. There are eight poems around to speak highly of this peculiar stone which is 3 meters in height, 3.5 meters in length. It is a relique of Mi Wanzhong, Ming Dynasty. After the first move to Yuanmingyuan, it was then moved here. Qingzhixiu stone and Qingyunpian stone are called a couple while the former is the husband and the later the wife.

青云片
Qingyunpian Stone

下篇 / 北京胡同风情游经典线路

Part B　Classical Travelling Routes to Beijing Hutong

北京胡同文化之旅
A CULTURE TOUR TO BEIJING HUTONG

一、东城区胡同游

　　东城区胡同旅游是以鼓楼为起点的。三轮车载着游客最先来到的是豆腐池胡同路北的杨昌济故居。这是一座小四合院。1918年夏天，毛泽东由湖南来京曾在这里住过一段时间。他在此看望老师，并领导了赴法勤工俭学运动。第二站行至方家胡同，游客可以观赏清代乾隆年间的循郡王府。这是座二进大四合院，三间一启的府门壮观而严肃。随后，来到成贤街，这是京城仅存的一条还保留有几座木牌楼的老街。在这里，路北有元、明、清三代最高学府国子监，院内有琉璃牌坊及辟雍亭。辟雍亭四面环水，优美雅静，是历史上皇帝讲学之处。再往前就是北京的孔庙（今为首都博物馆），院里大成殿气势非凡，历代帝王在这里祭祀孔子。今天这里还可以观赏大型祭孔表演。在这里还有碑林和元、明、清三代进士题名碑，至今保存完好。终点是雍和宫。雍和宫是京城最大的黄教喇嘛寺，其建筑风格独特，主殿中供养由一整块檀木雕成的18米高的大佛。东城区胡同游的另外一条路线是以钟楼为起点，

乘三轮车到南锣鼓巷地区，观赏元、明、清三代老胡同。这里有四进院落的总督府、婉容故居、齐白石故居、茅盾故居以及有特色的清代宅院、独特的拱门砖雕建筑和久负盛名的"可园"，可以了解四合院的生活和民风。

Hutong Tour in East District

  Hutong tour in East District starts from the Drum Tower, and then drives to the former residence of Yang Changji, aquadrangle, at the north road of Doufuchi Hutong by the pedicab. In the summer of 1918, Chairman Mao has lived here for a while after he left Hunan for Beijing to visit his teacher and later led a work-study movement in order to study in France. The second stop of this tour is the Mansion of Prince Xunjun, Qianlong times of Qing Dynasty, at Fangjia Hutong. The three-to-one type main gate looks grand and solemn, after which is a binary quadrangle. When finishing the visit of the mansion, we come to Chengxian Street which is one of the rare old streets where there is a wood archway. In the north road, there is Imperial College which is the highest school in Yuan, Ming and Qing Dynasties. Inside the college, there are a colored-glaze torri and a Piyong Pavilion. Surrounded by water, the pavilion is quiet and graceful which makes it the choice of many emperors where to deliever lectures. Confucius Temple, now the Capital Library, can be seen ahead. The extraordinary Dacheng Palace is the place where emperors made sacrifice to Confucius, the performance of which can still be watched today. Stele circles with the inscription of Jinshi of Yuan, Ming and Qing Dynasties are wellkept. The termination of this trip is Harony and Peace Palace Lamasery, the biggest Lama temple in Beijing which is specialized by the 18-meter Great Buddha, carved from a single trunk of white sandalwood in the main palace. The other route in this tour starts from the Drum Tower and then to the Nanluogu Street by pedicab to visit old Hutongs of Yuan, Ming and Qing Dynasties. Famous places in this route are: the Mansion of Viceroy, the former residence of Wanrong, the former residence of Qi Baishi, the former residence of Mao Dun, the Xanadu of Jiang Jieshi, Arch Brick Engravings and famed Ke Garden. The tourists can have a better understanding of lives and customs in quadrangles.

北京胡同文化之旅
A CULTURE TOUR TO BEIJING HUTONG

国子监辟雍亭（曾贻萱 摄）
Piyong Pavilion in Imperial College (by Zeng Yixuan)

国子监街一景
Imperial College Street

琉璃牌楼（李明智 摄）
Gate with coloured glaze (by Li Mingzhi)

国子监街　Imperial College Street

东城区胡同游的老街地段是国子监，清代称这里为成贤街。在这条街上巍然耸立着四座木牌楼，路两旁是古老的槐树。路北有始建于元代的孔庙和国子监，老街上还有保存完好的下马碑，上面用满汉文镌刻"文武官员到此下马"。路南至今还有一座明代的火神庙，街巷中还有多座老四合院，甚是幽静整洁。近年来，街面上出现了几处商店，展出、销售具有老北京特色的工艺品、玩具、旅游纪念品。老街以其古朴的景观和民风，吸引了众多的中外旅游者。这里是人力三轮车胡同游的主要景点。游人步行或乘车来这里观赏老街后，出东口往前就是京城著名的喇嘛庙——雍和宫。

The Imperial College Street is one of the spots in the Hutong tour in the East District which is originally named Chengxian Street. The four wooden gates are still standing on the street with old pagoda trees by the two sides of the road. The Confucius Temple and the Imperial College of Beijing locate in the north of the road. Dismounting stones are well-kept and the tourists can even recognize the script in Manchu and Han characters: civil and military officials are required to dismount here. In the south of the road, there is a Fire-fiend Temple of Ming Dynasty. Inside the street, there are many quiet and clean quadrangles standing there in peace. In recent years, several shops showed up in the old street, exhibiting of selling artworks, toys of souvenirs. The old street is attractive to tourists in and abroad

辟雍亭全景（李明智 摄）
Piyong Pavilion (by Li Mingzhi)

for its simplicity and original shape. Pedalcar Tours also choose here as an important sightseeing spot. After walking to or riding to this street, tourists can directly go east to the Lama Temple, the Harmony and Peace Palace Lamasey.

孔庙 Confucius Temple

孔庙位于成贤街路北，始建于元代。明永乐九年又重修了大成殿，清嘉庆九年为祭祀孔子五代先祖增建崇圣祠。乾隆二年皇帝亲谕孔庙使用黄琉璃瓦屋顶。庙内先师门两侧有数排石碑，是元、明、清三代进士题名碑。大成门内有石鼓10枚，上刻古诗，很有考证价值。今天这里是首都博物馆。

The Confucius Temple was built in Yuan Dynasty. In the 9th year of Yongle times, Ming Dynasty, the hall of Dacheng was rebuilt. In the 9th year of Jiaqing times, Qing Dynasty, Shrine of the Great Wise Man was built for the sacrifice of the five generations of Confucian ancestors. In the 2nd year of Qianlong times, the emperor instructed yellow

国子监街现存的下马碑
（张广太摄）
Dismounting Stele in Imperial College (by Zhang Guangtai)

北京孔庙
Confucions Temple in Beijing

coloerd-glaze to be used on the roof of the temple. At the two sides of the Xianshi Gate, there lines stone tablets which are Jinshi tablets of Yuan, Ming and Qing Dynasties.Inside the Gate of Dacheng, there are ten stone drums with poems carved on them. Now, it is the location of Capital Museum.

循郡王府　Mansion of Prince Xunjun

该府在方家胡同里，坐北朝南。循郡王名永璋，是乾隆皇帝第三子。这座三层大四合院，是典型的贝勒府的形制府第。近年进行了全部修缮，基本恢复了原貌。

This mansion lies in Fangjia Hutong, sitting at the north and facing the south. Prince Xunjun, named Yongzhang, is the third son of Emperor Qianlong. As a ternary quadrangle, it is a typical Beile mansion. The whole building has been restored to its origin .

循郡王府（李明智 摄）
Mansion of Prince Xunjun (by Li Mingzhi)

方家胡同小学（李明智 摄）
Fangjia Hutong Primary School (by Li Mingzhi)

方家胡同小学　Fangjia Hutong Primary School

循郡王府往东路北的方家胡同小学是所百年老校，著名作家老舍先生1918～1920年曾在这里任校长，那时该校名为"京师第十七国民及高等小学"。今天校门上的"方家胡同小学"六字是老舍夫人胡絜青女士生前所题。

Fangjia Hutong Primary School, sitting in the north road of Xunjun prince mansion, is an old school with over a hundred year's history. Laoshe, the famous writer, has been the principal of this school between 1918 and 1920, during which period the school is called the 17th National and Advanced Primary School of Beijing and inscription of Fangjia Hutong Primary School on the gate was the autography of Mrs. Hu Jieqing, wife of Laoshe.

毛主席故居　The Residence of Chairman Mao

在豆腐池胡同路北的毛主席故居，是一座两进小四合院。1918年杨昌济先生任北京大学教授时，全家在此居住。当年曾在门上挂"板仓杨寓"的铜牌。杨先生住里院北房，女儿杨开慧住外院，南屋为会客室。1918年8月毛泽东曾在这里居住，领导了赴法勤工俭学运动，并与杨开慧一起，在院中种下了一棵枣树。

This is a binary quadrangle where Mr. Yang Changji and his family lived when he was nominated the professor of Peking University in 1918. There was once a bronze board carved Ban-cang-yang-yu on the gate. Mr. Yang lived in the north room while his daughter Yang Kaihui lived in the outer room and the south room was used as the assembly room. Chairman Mao lived here since August, 1918 when he led the Work-study Program to France. There is also a Chinese jujube in the yard which is planted by Chairman Mao and Yang Kaihui.

方家胡同 13 号旧宅院　Old House in No.13 Fangjia Hutong

这是一组清代大四合院，原为循郡王府的一部分，但清末又重新改建。主院的北房和东西配房，均有廊子相通，古树、假山石相映成趣。清光绪时，出使德国的状元洪钧回京后，与妾赛金花在此院居住过。

毛主席故居
The residence of Mr.Yang Changji (Former Residence of Chairman Mao)

该院的广亮大门门楼（张广太 摄）
Guangliang gate of the courtyard (by Zhang Guangtai)

This is a quadrangle of Qing Dynasty and it was originally part of Mansion of Prince Xunjun. It has been reconstructed in late Qing. Corridors connect the north room and east & west side rooms in the main courtyard, decorated by old trees and rockery. When Number One Scholar Hongjun came back from Germany, he and his concubine Saijinhua has lived here.

雍和宫牌楼前
Gate of Harmony and Peace Palace Lamasery

雍和宫
Harmony and Peace Palace Lamasery

这里是京城最大、保存最好的喇嘛黄教寺院。建筑融汉藏艺术为一体，主殿内供奉高 18 米的大佛，是一整块白檀木所雕成。在此处，还可以欣赏到俗称"打鬼"的"跳布扎"的壮观场面。

This is the biggest and best-kept Lama temple in Beijing. The whole building is a combination of Han architecture and Tibetan architecture. Inside the main palace, there is an eighteen-meter Buddha carved from a single trunk of white sandalwood. Besides the culture connotation, tourists have a chance to witness the traditional Tiaobuzha performance which means expelling the ghosts.

国祥胡同 2 号四合院
The Quadrangle in No.2 Guoxiang Hutong

此地原是清代的那王府。原院落很大，现仅存两个四合院。其古建很有特色，东院的垂花门、西厢房为两卷勾连搭式的过厅。垂花门处有走廊可通向西院，院内有后罩房七间，花草丛生，屋前有两座太湖石，更增添了几分典雅。

This was the former Na Prince Mansion in Qing Dynasty with a big courtyard which has left two quadrangles only today. The architecture is very special here especially for the festoon door of

万福阁内供奉木雕迈达拉佛，相传是由一根 20 余米的白檀香木雕塑成的
The wooden Mailada Buddha in Wanfu pavilion is said to be carved by a twenty-meter white sandal wood.

the east yard and the hall of west side-house with Goulianda roof. There is a corridor leading to the west yard from the festoon door. Passing the corridor, seven back rooms dotted by prosperous flowers, together with the Tai Lake Stone in front of the room, compose a beautiful scene.

古刹白衣庵　Baiyi Nunnery

位于方家胡同路北的古刹白衣庵始建于明代，山门三间，有四层殿宇和跨院。原庵内供奉观音像及九尊娘娘像，还保存有清道光年间刻制的兰亭镇水刻石七方。新中国成立后，这里还保持着佛事活动。"文革"开始后佛像被毁，殿堂均成了居民住房。今天，该庵山门上仍可见"古刹白衣庵"五字，院内多层殿宇尚存，檐柱虽很破旧，可庆幸的是还可以看到古刹建筑原貌。

老宅院一角
Corner of the old residence

古刹白衣庵的山门局部（李明智 摄）
Gate of Baiyi Nunnery (details, by Li Mingzhi)

古刹白衣庵（李明智 绘）
Baiyi nunnery (painted by Li Mingzhi)

Baiyi nunnery, lying in north road of Fangjia Hutong, was first built in Ming dynasty, which includes three frontispieces, four-layered palaces and courtyards. There once was the statuary of Kwanyin and nine statuary of the Goddess and carving stone from Lanting county which is carved in Daoguang Year. After the liberation, Buddhist ceremony and activities are still available here. Dur-ing the Cultural Revolution, statuaries were destroyed and the palace came to be the residence of the local people. Today, we can still view the script of the name of the nunnery on the gate and the multi-layer palaces are all the same kept although the roofs and columns have been deformed. Fortunately, we have the honor to see the original face of the ancient nunnery.

南锣鼓巷　NANLUOGU LANE

东城区的南锣鼓巷是一条南北向的长街巷，南头是地安门东大街，北端是鼓楼东大街。在这条长巷中，东西对称的胡同有 16 条，连同主街形成了蜈蚣状，老百姓称之为蜈蚣巷。从明、清两代保留下的地图资料看，这些胡同形成于元代，经过数百年的风云变化，今天依然保存原样；至于胡同的名称也大部分为老名字，其建筑风貌更保持着老街道的特点。这里的胡同内不同类型的四合院门楼整齐，有的老宅院门前还保存着上下马石和雕刻完美的抱鼓石。这是胡同文化的实物写照，另外还有现存的众多文物保护单位（名人故居、清代的宅第和园林）。清代该地区满族镶黄旗住户为多，有官宦之家，也有众多的小户民居。那时，南锣鼓巷街面上商店很全，饽饽铺、茶叶铺、粮店、酒店、当铺、饭馆、猪肉扛、菜店……可谓店铺俱全。胡同内均为民居，从未开设商户，百姓们在此地区生活得安宁和谐。改革开放以来，自20世纪90年代中期，南锣鼓巷出现了各类商店，如有京城特色的奶酪店、书店、酒吧等。胡同旅游的三轮车来到了老街巷，众多的中外旅游者对这里的四合院和民俗深感兴趣，在街巷中留下他们的足迹。

Nanluogu Lane is a south-north lane which links the east Avenue of Di'an Gate at the south end and the east Avenue of Drum Tower at the north end. Sixteen Hutongs locates symmetrically at the east and west which constitutes a map of scolopendra and that is why the lane is called the scolopendra lane by the locals. According to the records of maps of Ming and Qing Dynasties, the Hutongs came into being in Yuan Dynasty but remained its origin through the long history. Even the name of the Hutongs keeps it old call, no matter the feature of the old streets. All the diversified quadrangles are in order, in front of some of which there are stepping stones and fine works of drum piers. As a historical portraiture of Hutong culture in Beijing, you can also find many cultural relics such as the former residence of celebrities, mansions and gardens in Qing Dynasty. In Qing Dynasty, most of the residents of this area are Xianghuangqi of Manchu, including both rich merchants and the civilians. Almost all kinds of shops can be found in the Nanluogu Lane, such as bun shop, tea shop, foodstuff shop, groggery, pawnshop, restaurant, pork store and vegetable shop. However, inside the dozen of the Hutongs, there has never been any store and only the populace lived here in peace and harmony. Since the Reform and Open movement, especially after the middle of 1990s, Nanluogu Lane is enriched by various stores such as famous Beijing cheese store, bookstore and pub. The pedal car shows the foreign visitors around, down into the quadrangles and the national culture and customs are extremely attractive to the tourists.

总督府（黑芝麻胡同 13 号）
Mansion of Viceroy in No. 13 Heizhima Hutong

  此院是清代四川总督奎俊的府第，共有五进院落，门楼前有上马石一对，大门洞内有抱鼓石一对，其雕刻古朴大方。院里的垂花门、抄手廊都很具特色，是典型的多进大四合院。

  This is the residence of Sichuan viceroy Kuijun, Qing Dynasty. There are two mounting stones in front of the gate and a pair of Drum Piers inside the gate, the carving of which is simple but elegant. Quinary quadrangle as it is, this mansion is typically a huge multi-tier courtyard. The festoon door and corridors are both designed finely.

文煜故居 The Former Residence of Wenyu

  帽儿胡同 11 号，是清代大学士文煜的宅第。这是一座五进院落，布局严谨，屋宇高大，庭院宽敞，原为文煜所建。北洋政府时期冯国璋居此。

  This is the residence of Great Scholar Wenyu, Qing Dynasty. This is a quinary quadrangle which is tall in room-design and wide in courtyard. It was built by Wenyu first and then came to be the residence of Feng Guozhang in Beiyang times.

总督府近照（李海川摄）
A close view at the Governor's Mansion (by Li Haichuan)

文煜故居
The former residence of Wenyu

婉蓉故居
The former resideme of Wanrong

婉蓉故居正房中精美的木雕落地罩
Delicate wooden floor-lamp cover in the main room of the former residence of Wanrong

婉容故居（帽儿胡同 35 号）
The Former Residence of Wanrong (No. 35 Mao'er Hutong)

这座旧宅院是清朝末代皇帝溥仪的皇后婉容的旧居，原为婉容曾祖父郭布罗长顺所建。婉容被册封皇后以后，其父升为内务府大臣，封为三等承恩公。现西院建筑完好，四进院落，东路为三进，有月亮门、假山、祠堂等。后院正房三间，室内还保存着一面巨大的镜子，是清代由国外购置的，婉容在入宫之前，每日在镜前演习礼仪。今天这面巨镜已成了文物。

This is the former residence of Empress Wanrong of the last Emperor Puyi of Qing Dynasty, which was built by the great-grandfather of Wanrong, Guobuluochangshun. When she was selected as the empress, her father was promoted as the minister of Imperial Household Department, a 3rd rank Cheng'en-gong. The two yards are wellkept today. The east route is ternary with Moon Gate, rockery and ancestral temple, while there are three main rooms at the back yard, inside which a huge mirror imported from the abroad was put. Before Wanrong was selected, she practiced royal manner in front of this mirror. And today, the mirror has become a cultural relic.

文昌帝君庙　The Temple of Emperor Wenchang

在帽儿胡同西口路北有一条小巷，这里有个老院子，原是明代成化十三年（1477 年）

始建的文昌帝君庙，百姓称它为梓庙。原建有山门、钟鼓二楼正殿，供文昌帝君像。文昌帝君是主管文运之神。现在仅存大殿为居民所住，院内还保存着一座巨碑，通高4米，上有清嘉庆皇帝撰文、乾隆年间大学士刘墉所书碑记，记述该庙的历史，历经200余年仍保存完好，尤为珍贵。近前观赏，其碑上所刻的楷书字清晰可辨。

Down to the lane in the north road of the west entrance of Mao'er Hutong, there is an old courtyard which is the temple of Emperor Wenchang first built in the 13th Chenghua Year in Ming Dynasty (1477 A. D.). The local people call it the Zitong Temple. There used to be a frontispiece, a drum tower and bell tower with the statuary of Emperor Wenchang, the God in charge of the achievements in culture and education. However, the only kept main palace has turned out to be the residence of the locals. But there is a huge stele standing in the middle of the yard which is four meters in height. The words on the stele tell the history of the temple which is initiated by Emperor Qianlong and written by the Scholar Liu Yong. This stele is of great value and importance as a cultural relic since it is wll-reserved after the baptism of over two hundred years. The words carved on the stele can even be clearly seen with a close look at.

齐白石故居　The Former Residence of Qi Baishi

雨儿胡同13号，原为清代内务府总管大臣的宅第。新中国建立后，著名国画家齐白石曾住在这里，后在此建立齐白石纪念馆。该院为二层大四合院，其建筑很有特色。进里院带转角廊，此屋明间木隔扇上刻有对联："本书以求其质，本诗以求其情，本礼以求其宜，本易以求其道；勿展无益之卷，勿吐无益之话，勿涉无益之境，勿近无益之人。"横额："乐生于智，寿本乎仁。"此等佳句可使人们读后深思。

No. 13 of Yu'er Hutong is the former residence of general minister of Imperial Household Department. Famed artist Qi Baishi lived here once after 1949 and then it is turned to be the Memorial to Qi Baishi. This is a binary quadrangle which is different in the crossing corridor in each yard. There is a couplet on the

文昌帝君庙院内保存完好的石碑
Well-kept stele inside the yard of the temple of Emperor Wenchang

齐白石故居
The former residence of Qi Baishi

茅盾故居
Former residence of Mr.Mao Dun

wood door: Reading books for its connotation, enjoying poems for its passion, behaving polite for fine relation, being simple for its Tao; rejecting the worthless books, dumbing for meaningless words, removing from the profitless environment, keeping aloof from the virtueless people. The banner in the middle is Happiness derived from wisdom, longevity rooted in benevolence. The sentences do make people deliberate.

茅盾故居 The Former Residence of Mao Dun

该故居位于后圆恩寺胡同路北，是一座三进的清末老四合院。茅盾，原名沈德鸿，字雁冰，浙江桐乡人。中国现代进步文化的先驱，伟大的革命文学家，卓越的无产阶级文化战士。他从1916年开始从事文学活动，对我国新文化运动产生了巨大影响。新中国成立后，任文化部部长、全国文联副主席。茅盾创作了《子夜》《蚀》《春蚕》《林家铺子》《虹》等文化作品。1974年12月茅盾与其子居住在这里，直至1981年3月病逝。在这个院子里，有先生生前的起居室和工作室，陈设全是旧物，保留原貌。在前院立塑像，辟有展室。

The house locates in the north road of the Temple of Houyuan'en, a trinary quadrangle of the late Qing Dynasty. Mr. Mao Dun, the original name of whom is Shen Dehong was born in Tongxiang, Zhejiang province. He is a pioneer of Chinese modern culture, a great revolutionist and litterateur and an outstanding proletarian soldier. Mr. Mao devoted himself

起居室一角
Corner of the living-room

茅盾故居院内一景
Spot in the courtyard of the former residence of Mao Dun

into cultural activities in 1916 and had great influence on national new cultural movement. After the founding of PRC, he worked as the minister of national Ministry of Culture and the vice president of China Federation of Literature and Art Circles. He produced the famous works such as Midnight, Erosion, Spring Silkworm, the Store of Lin's and the Rainbow. Mr. Mao and his son have lived here since December, 1974 and not until March, 1981 that Mr. Mao passed away here. The living room and workroom are still kept in order with the old staff in exhibition. The statuary of Mr. Mao Dun was erected in the front courtyard and the special exhibition room for him is open to the pulic.

可园　Ke Garden

这里是清末大学士文煜的旧宅花园。原主人的住宅与花园相通，现已隔开。花园部分很美。进门经过弯曲小径，直通假山，山洞上刻"幽径"二字。走过山洞，眼前豁然开朗，往北可见正房五间，往东过小桥又到亭台，此处较高，可放眼全园。太湖石旁有石碑一座，上刻"可园"二字。游廊依地势而建，又通向后园，加之园内四季树木，花草丛丛，甚是优美典雅。

　　This is the garden of the old mansion of the Great Scholar Wenyu, Qing Dynasty. It was originally linked with the mansion, but was separated now. Along the winding paths, you come to a rockery with words Youjing carved on the cavern. Going through the

可园内景（之一）
A Scence in the Ke Garden

可园内景（之二）
A Scence in the Ke Garden

可园一景
Spot of the Ke Garden

可园一景（手绘）
Spot of the Ke Garden

cavern, you will have a wide vision at once. There are five main rooms to the north and a pavilion across a bridge to the east. The pavilion stands at a higher position where you can have a outlook of the whole garden. By the Tai Lake Stone, there is a stele carved Ke Garden. Corridors built delicately according to the change of the hypsography, together with the green trees and blooming flowers, turns out a nice picture.

棉花胡同 15 号拱门砖雕
Arch Brick Engravings of No.15 Mianhua Hutong

在棉花胡同 15 号院内，一座砖雕精美的拱门呈现在眼前。此门为拱形，高 5 米，宽 3 米，从门洞两旁的金刚墙至栏板，均雕刻文字和松、竹、梅、多宝阁等图案，其布局严谨，刀工精美。此拱门和院内的垂花门都是清代建筑。

The arch brick engraving locates in the No. 15 Mianhua Hutong. The arch door is five meters in height and three meters in width. From the Jingang Wall to the parapet, there are delicate carving characters and flowers as cypress, bamboo, clubs and cornucopia. The arch door and the festoon door inside the yard are both Qing architecture.

拱门局部雕刻（刘松年 摄）
Exquisite arch gate (by Lu Songnian)

板厂胡同 27 号四合院
Quadrangle in No. 27 Banchang Hutong

这是一座保存完好的三进四合院，门内有砖雕影壁，外院倒座房六间。走进垂花门，呈现抄手游廊；正房三间，左右各有耳房两间；经月亮门可转至后院，后罩房七间。此宅院为清代建筑，很有晚清庭院特色。

This is a well-kept ternary quadrangle. There are a brick carving screen wall inside the gate and six inverse side-rooms in the outer yard. Stepping into the festoon door, there is the Chaoshou Corridor. By the two sides of the three main rooms, there are two ear-rooms. You can get to the back yard through the Moon Gate and there are seven Houzhao rooms there. This is a Qing building and even today, we can still find the feature of the courtyards of late Qing.

砖雕精细、造型独特的拱门（刘松年 摄）
Exquisite arch gate (by Lu Songnian)

板厂胡同 27 号四合院
Quadrangle in NO.27 Banchang Hutong

荣禄故宅（张广太 摄）
The resident of Ronglu (by Zhang Guangtai)

蒋介石行辕部分景观（刘松年 摄）
Part of the temporary residence of Jiang Jieshi (by Liu Songnian)

荣禄故宅　The Resident of Ronglu

菊儿胡同3号旧宅院，这里是清光绪时直隶总督荣禄的宅第。大门坐北朝南，院内月台上正房五间及东西厢房均为清代建筑，至今保存完好。

The residential No.3 in Ju'er Hongtong is the mansion of Zhili Viceroy, Ronglu, in Guangxu time of Qing Dynasty. It's on the north and to the south. The five room on the platform in the yard and the west and east side-room are Qing buildings and are kept well.

后圆恩寺胡同7号老宅院
Quadrangle in No.7 Houyuan'ensi Hutong

此院原是清代庆亲王之子的宅第。除正规的老四合院建筑之外，还有一座西洋式的小楼房和花园。抗战胜利后，这里是国民党政府总统蒋介石的行辕。新中国成立后，该处为中国共产党华北局所在地。今天此院为友好宾馆，迎来了大批中外旅游者。

This is the mansion of the second son of Prince YiKuang, Qing Dynasty. The whole building has an old quadrangle as well as a western-style storied building and a garden. After the success of the anti-Japanese War, it became the Xanadu of the president of Kuomintang, Jiang Jieshi. When China was liberated by the CPC, it came to be Huabei Bureau of CPC. Today, it is Youhao Hotel which has been open to tourists around the world.

钟楼　Bell Tower

钟楼在鼓楼北边，是中轴线上最北端的古建筑。该楼高47.95米，全部结构是砖石材料，悬挂在楼上的铜钟是明永乐年

京城的钟楼（刘金城摄）
Bell Tower (by Liu Jincheng)

楼上的大钟（李海川摄）
The bell on the tower (by Li Haichuan)

间所铸造。清代是昼夜报时，乾隆以后改为夜间报更两次。第一次是在晚上7时为"定更"，第二次是早晨5时，称为"亮鼓"。钟、鼓楼上的更夫在报时之前，相互将手中的"孔明灯"对照，作为信号，然后分别进入楼中击鼓、撞钟。

The Bell Tower lies to the north of the Drum Tower as one of the ancient architecture in the central axis at the northern point. The tower, made of brick and stone, is 47.95 meters in height; the bronze bee hanging upstairs was cast during Yongle Year, Ming Dynasty. The day-and-night tolling in Qing Dynasty was altered to twice tolling during the night by Emperor Qianglong, the first of which is at seven O'clock in the evening and the second at five in the morning. The bellman on the Bell Tower and the Drum Tower carried a Kongming lamp each and by shining and notifying each other, they enter the different tower to toll the bell and play the drum.

鼓楼　Drum Tower

该楼建在京城的中轴线上，巍峨壮观，令人瞩目。二层上设更鼓，鼓面直径1.5米，用整张牛皮蒙制。明、清两代为京城报时，晚7时为"定更"，击鼓两通，击

京城鼓楼近照（刘永顺 摄）
Drum Tower (by Lin Yongshun)

鼓楼上的击鼓表演
Drum Show on Drum Tower

108下，以后每次再击鼓。直至五更，即晨5时为最后"亮鼓"。今天这里对外开放，每天均有击鼓表演。

The magnificent tower lies on the axis of the city of Beijing. There is a huge drum made of a complete piece of cowhide on the second floor which is 1.5 meters in diameter. It is used to give the time to the public during the Ming and Qing Dynasties. At seven O'clock in the evening, the drum will be beaten for twice, 108 sounds in total. At five O'clock in the morning, the drum will be beaten again to declare the rise of the sun. Today, there are still drumbeaten show and bell-tolling show everyday.

地安门古桥 Di'an Gate Bridge

该桥在地安门外大街上，始建于元代，名为万宁桥。因地安门又称后门，因此称为后门桥。近年进行了全面修缮，是一座单孔石桥，桥下岸边有镇水兽一对，石雕精美壮观。

The bridge locates on the street of Di'an Gate, first built in Yuan Dynasty. The original name of the bridge is Wanning bridge. Since Di'an Gate is also called the Back Gate and the bridge can also be called the Back Gate bridge. The singe-hole stone bridge has been completely restored recently. Under the bridge, there are a pair of protection beasts whose carving technique is finery and brilliant.

古老的后门桥
Old Back-door Bridge

文天祥祠（刘松年 摄）
Wen Tianxiang Ancestral Temple (by Liu Songnian)

文天祥祠　Wen Tianxiang Ancestral Temple

该祠坐落在鼓楼东大街交道口南的府学胡同里，始建于明洪武九年，乃为纪念我国南宋民族英雄文天祥而立，俗称文丞相祠。文天祥被元军掳至大都（今北京），在这里的土牢中，写下了不朽之作《正气赋》，后被杀害在柴市。现堂房内有明代石碑，上刻《宋文丞相传》，两壁镶有"教忠坊"石刻匾。院内有一颗古枣树，为文天祥亲手所植。

The ancestral temple locates in the Fuxue Hutong in the south of Jiaodaokou near the Drum Tower. It was first built in the 9th of Hongwu time in Ming Dynasty in memory of Wen Tianxiang, the national hero of Nan Song Dynasty. Mr. Wen was captived by the Yuan soldiers to Dadu (Beijing), where he produced his famous works, the Fugue for righteousness. The stone-carving plaques are inlayed on both walls and the old Chinese jujube in the yard was planted by Wen Tianxiang himself.

顺天府学　Shuntian Government College

文丞相祠西侧是明洪武年间所建的顺天府学，这里有明代"学制碑"和大成殿，清代为顺天学政。今天已将原古建进行了全面修复，是府学胡同小学所在地。

Shuntian Government College lies in the west of the ancestral temple of Wen prime

魁星门一景
Kuixing Gate

院内一景
Corner of the quadrangle

府学院内一角
Corner of Shuntian Government College

老舍故居（刘松年 摄）
Former residence of Mr. Laoshe (by Liu Songnian)

minister. It was constructed in Hongwu times in Ming Dynasty and the stele of Educational System and Dacheng Palace of Ming Dynasty are still visible today. In Qing Dynasty, the educational system is Shuntian system. After a complete restoration of the ancient architecture, this site today is the location of Fuxue Hutong Elementary School.

老舍故居　The Former Residence of Mr. Laoshe

老舍故居在东城区灯市口西街丰富胡同 19 号，是一座老四合院，自 1950 年 3 月老舍先生全家迁至此院居住。这里北院的正房、西耳房就是先生的书房和工作室。园中的柿子树，就是先生和夫人胡絜青一起种下的，此院又称为丹柿小院。老舍（1890~1966 年），现代小说家、戏剧家。原名舒庆春，字舍予，北京人。早年曾任英国伦敦大学东方学院教员、齐鲁大学和山东大学教授。新中国成立后任中国文联副主席、中国作家协会副主席、北京市文联主席。一生创作长篇小说 16 部，短篇小说 70 余篇，剧本 36 个，诗歌、曲艺、杂文约 1400 余篇，被授予"人民艺术家"称号。

The house locates in the 19th of Fengfu Hutong, the west street of Dengshixikou, the East District. It is an old quadrangle and comes to be the residence of Mr. Laoshe since March 1950. the main room and the west side-room in the north yard are used for study and workroom. The persimmon in the garden was planted by Mr. Laoshe and his wife Mrs. Hu Jieqing and that is the reason why the yard is also named the persimmon garden. Mr. Laoshe (1890 ~ 1966), the famous Beijing novelist and player-writer, was first named Shu Qingchun when he was born. He has been the teacher in the Oriental College of London university and professor in Qilu university and Shandong university. After the Liberation, he has been the vice president of China Federation of Literature and Art Circles, vice president of Chinese Writers Association and the president of Beijing Municipal Federation of Literature and Art Circles. During his life, he produced sixteen saga novels, over seventy short stories, thirty-six plays and over fourteen hundred poems and scribbles. He was honored as People's Artist.

二、西城区胡同游（北线）

这项旅游起程点在什刹海，游客乘坐车棚上有"胡同旅游"四个大字的人力三轮车，可以观赏素有京城西湖之称的什刹海景区，附近还有燕京八景之一"银锭观山"。站在京城古老的银锭桥上，天气晴朗的时候，可以看到西山。行至柳荫街，可以看到老北京四合院有特色的如意门和门槛两旁石雕精美、造型独特的门墩。还可以随导游走进百姓家，与居民聊天，或吃顿家常饭，外宾还可以学到包饺子的手艺。往前行又来到书画社，在这里可以现场欣赏书画家挥毫泼墨。这里还展卖北京特色的工艺品、玩具等，可让游客大饱眼福。沿途可以参观郭沫若故居和清代的恭王府花园。恭王府里可以登假山、观水榭、品茶、到老戏楼欣赏京剧和各种曲艺，别是一番风味。走出王府，游客接乘三轮车沿后海北河沿至宋庆龄故居。该院原是清朝大学士明珠的宅第，既有古建亭台，又有楼房，花木繁茂，甚是典雅。新中国建立以后，宋庆龄自1963年迁来此地居住办公，直到逝世。游客在这里可以看到她生前办公的地方和卧室，以及她珍藏的纪念品。参观完毕，继续乘坐三轮车可以沿南官房、东官房等老胡同返回出发地。

西城胡同游首发地（李明德摄）
Starting point of West District tour (by Li Mingde)

Hutong Tour in West District(North Route)

This tour starts from the Shichahai by pedicab with Hutong Tour on the shed. In this route, you have the chance to sightsee many famous scenic spots around Shichahai, including one of the Eight Spots in Yanjing (old name of Beijing), the Mountain Vision from Yinding Bridge. When it is clear and sunny, you can see the West Mountain from the bridge. In Liuyin Street, there are traditional Beijing quadrangles and special Ruyi Gate, as well as the stone piers with engravings on by the gate. Followed by the tour guide, tourists can visit people living in Hutong, chatting or having dinner with them. Foreign guests can also learn to make dumplings here. The next stop is a painting house where tourists are able to witness artists drawing on the spot. Artworks and all kinds of toys are available here too. The former residence of Guo Moruo and the garden of the Mansion of Prince Yixin, Qing Dynasty, are on the way. In the prince mansion, tourists can not only enjoy the beautiful rockery and fine tea, but watch an opera performance here. Along the west bank of Shichahai, pedicab will lead us to the former residence of Song Qingling which is originally the mansion of the Great Scholar Mingzhu, Qing Dynasty. The complete architecture is very elegant, with oldstyle pavilion and modern building. Ms. Song moved here since 1963 and worked here until she died. Tourists can visit her former office, bedroom as well as many precious souvenirs. After visiting here, pedicab will take us back to the starting point by way of Nanguanfang and Dongguanfang.

什刹海　Shichahai Sea

这里是京城的一片水域,为明清时期外三海(即前海、后海、积水潭)之一,因岸上有座古刹"什刹海寺"而得名。夏日三海荷花盛开,沿岸绿柳如烟,人们都赶至湖畔赏荷纳凉,可谓京城消夏的自然园林。北岸、南岸自古就有茶棚和店铺。今天,附近又开办了荷花市场,还有多处有特色的酒吧,是京城一处旅游胜地。

The water area of Beijing was called Three Outer Sea during Ming and Qing Dynasties, the Front Sea, the Back Sea and Jishuitan. It is named Shichahai because of the old temple, Shichahai Temple on the bank. In the summer day, blooming lotus on the water with the green willow along the bank, make up of a beautiful natural landscape. Tea house and stores on the north and south bank have existed for a long time. Today, a Lotus Market is open to tourists. Together with many distinctive pubs, here is a new scenic spot of Beijing.

北海公园　Beihai Park

该公园始建于金,那时为皇帝的行宫,其历史已有900余年。元世祖忽必烈又在这里的琼华岛上兴建宫殿。明代在此基础上有所扩建,山上筑白塔,湖面立亭台。清

什刹海前的荷花市场
Lotus market by Shichahai

湖面宽阔的什刹海
Shicha Sea

乾隆时在山的西侧立碑，皇帝题"琼岛春阴"四字并写下御制诗，因此此处成为"燕京八景"之一。东岸的画舫斋，桥廊相连，别具一格。北海公园是全国文物保护单位，是旅游观光的胜地。

It was built during Jin Dynasty which has had a history over nine hundred years. At that time, there had been a Xanadu for the emperor, but Hubilie, the emperor of Yuan Dynasty built another palace on the Qionghua Island. A continuation was built in Ming Dynasty, then there is the white pagoda on the hill and pavilions above the water. During Qing Dynasty, Emperor Qianlong erected a stele at the west side of the hill with the inscription Qiong Island Spring. This is one of the Eights Scenic Spots of Peking. On the east bank, bridges and corridors are connected to a fantastic gallery. Beihai Park is one of the national cultural relic of preservation spots and it is also the most popular scenic spot in Beijing.

北海公园
Beihai Park

古老的烟袋斜街　Old Yandai Diagonal Street

在鼓楼前路西，有一条北京最老的斜街，名叫烟袋斜街。该街建于明朝初年，街的走向和地形很奇特，加之明、清时期以至民国，斜街上有多家店铺专营烟袋，故此得名。这里的烟袋铺台阶较高，门前还挂起3尺来长的巨形烟袋当幌子，黑色的烟袋杆，黄铜的烟袋锅儿，还系着红布条。喜欢抽烟的人们，经常到这里选购烟袋。今天，在这条老街上，还会见到不少老的店铺，但已经没有经营烟业的门面了，原来的木制大烟袋幌子早就消失了。有特色的工艺品商店、古玩玉器商店、酒吧、餐厅、洗浴各类店铺林立于街巷两旁，形成了民俗风味很浓的步行街，受到了中外旅游者的欢迎。古老的斜街又焕发了青春。

烟袋斜街上有特色的店铺
Distinctive store in Yandai Diagonal Street

烟袋斜街路北老店铺一景
Old store in Yandai Diagonal Lane

繁华的烟袋斜街
Busy Yandai Diagonal Lane

烟袋斜街路北的古刹
Old temple at the north Yandai Diagonal Lane

To the west road of the Drum Tower, there is the oldest diagonal street in Beijing, the Yandai Diagonal Street. The street was built in the early years of Ming Dynasty and then was named so because of its special terrain and various stores selling the China tobacco pipes. The terrace of those stores is pretty high and a huge tobacco pipe was erected as a signboard, which is made a black pipestem and yellow bronze holder with a red leftover. People who have addiction for the cigarette, are frequent visitor here. Today, we can still find plenty of old stores, however, those for tobacco pipes have gone with the wooden pipe signboard. The walking commercial street now is enriched by stores of technical works, curio store, bar, restaurant and public bathroom. It becomes a hot spot for tourists for its sterling folk culture.

郭沫若故居　The Former Residence of Guo Moruo

这里原为清乾隆时权相和珅的花园，民国时又是辅仁大学的一部分。新中国成立后，曾是蒙古人民共和国驻华使馆。1963年全国文联主席、中国科学院院长郭沫若同志来此宅居住，至1978年去世。今天已对外开放。正房是郭老生前的会客室、办公室和卧室，后罩房是郭老夫人于立群女士的画室和书房。院西侧还有展室，陈列郭老手稿和藏书。

This was originally the garden of Heshen in Qianlong times, Qing Dynasty and it was part of Furen University during the Republic of China.

郭沫若故居
The former residence of Mr.Guo Moruo

After the People's Republic China was founded, it came to be the embassy of Mongolia Republic. In 1963, Mr. Guo Moruo, chairman of China Federation of Literature and Art Circles and the president of Chinese Academy of Sciences came to live here until he died in 1978. Today, it is open to tourists. The main rooms are the meeting hall, working place and bedroom of Mr. Guo while the back rooms are studio and study of Mrs. Guo, Yu Liqun. There are exhibition rooms at the west side which is used to exhibit the drafts and books of Mr. Guo.

广福观　Guangfu Taoist Temple

此观在烟袋斜街路北，始建于明代。现保存山门三间，石门额上刻有"广福观"三字。院内有前殿和后殿及东西配殿，并立有大明天顺年间重修广福观碑。

The temple locates in the north road of Yandai diagonal street which was first built in Ming Dynasty. Three frontispieces are still visible today with the script of Guangfu Taoist Temple on it. There is a front palace, back palace and side palaces to the east and west. There is also a temple stele standing rebuilt in Tianshun Year in Ming Dynasty.

宋庆龄故居　The Former Residence of Song Qingling

该府第原为清初大学士明珠的住处，现为中华人民共和国名誉主席宋庆龄同志故居。宋庆龄同志自 1963 年来此居住，内宅建有前厅"濠梁乐趣"和后厅"畅襟斋"。宋庆龄同志曾在这里多次与国家领导人共同讨论国家大事，还在这里会见、宴请外宾。今天这里是宋庆龄生平展览室。二楼是她的办公室和卧室。楼外西北角有"鸽子房"，在这里游人可以看到宋庆龄同志生前饲养的鸽子至今仍在此栖息。院内还有扇形建筑"箑亭"和"听雨屋"等，已辟为陈列室，展出宋庆龄珍藏的纪念品。

This was first the residence of the Great Scholar Mingzhu of early Qing and now it is the former residence of Song Qingling, the honorary chairman of People's Republic of China. Ms. Song came to live here since 1963. There is a front hall, the Haoliang- lequ and the back hall, the Changjinzhai. It is in this residence that Ms. Song met leaders of China and discussed the state affairs and it is also in this residence that she interviewed the foreign

宋庆龄故居
The former residence of Song Qingling

宋庆龄故居内
The former residence of Song Qingling

剑石
Sword-shaped stone

园内长廊
Corridor in the garden

起居室与会客厅
Sitting room and meeting room

leaders and guests. Today, it is the exhibition hall of Song's daily life. The office and bed room are on the second floor. The pigeon house is at the northwest corner outside the tower where tourists can still see the pigeons Ms. Song fed. The fan-shaped halls have all turned to be exhibition halls of souvenir of Song.

醇亲王府　Chunqin Mansion

府邸位于后海北岸，坐北朝南，原为清初大学士明珠的府邸，至光绪时赐给醇亲王奕。府内建筑分三路，中路有过厅和正殿，后面还有九间后罩楼。现府内建筑完好，甚是壮观。

The mansion at the north of Houhai locates at the north and to the south. It was the mansion of great scholar Mingzhu and obliged to Chunqin, Yixuan in Guangxu year of Qing Dynasty. The buildings of the mansion includes three pathway. Behind the midway of pass room and main hall, there are nine Houzhao rooms. Now the well-kept spectacular buildings are in the list municipal cultural protection units.

五间三启门的醇亲王府（张广太摄）
Chunqin Mansion with five-to-three gate (by Zhang Guangtai)

恭王府　Mansion of Prince Yixin

该府坐北朝南，为三开一启门。府前有石狮子一对，进二门后是正殿，称为"嘉乐堂"。东路有"多福轩"和"乐道堂"，西路有"葆光室"和"锡晋斋"。后院有二层后罩楼环抱，共计50余间。整个府第建筑保持着清乾隆时的特征，环境幽美。这里原是清道光皇帝第六子恭亲王奕訢府邸。

The mansion stands at the north and faces the south and it is a three-to-one gate quadrangle. There is a pair of stone lions in front of the first gate and the main palace, Jiale Hall, shows up after the second gate. The Duofu Room and Ledao Hall are at the east road while the Baoguang Hall and Xijin Room at the west. The back yard is surrounded by a two-storied tower which has more than fifty rooms in all. The whole architecture still keeps the features of Qing Dynasty. This was originally the residence of Prince Yixin, the sixth son of Emperor Daoguang, Qing Dynasty.

蝙蝠厅
Hall of bats

恭王府花园 Garden of the Mansion of Prince Yixin

　　这里是恭王府的花园部分，近年已经对外开放。此园原名萃锦园，坐北朝南，是西洋式石雕花拱券门。进园是一块巨大的太湖石，刻有"独乐峰"三字。后面是呈蝙蝠形的池水和错落叠成的大片假山石。内有秘云洞，供有清康熙帝御笔"福"字碑。高处建有"邀月"厅，左右有爬山廊，最后是造型独特的"蝠殿"。东院还建有三卷勾连搭式大戏楼一座。湖心亭又称之水榭。在花园西侧，水面上又筑石舫一座，是历代园主垂钓之处。假山东侧的流杯亭建筑很有特色，亭中地面刻有宽槽，引来清水，可邀客人围坐于亭内，放酒杯于水道中，杯漂至停处，客人即赋诗，以达"曲水流觞"之乐。观赏此亭，别具风趣。园内松柏苍翠，古木参天，鸟语花香。

　　This is the Cuijin Garden of the prince mansion which is open to tourists today. The arch gate with flower engraving of western style stands at the north and faces the south. Entering the gate, there is a huge Tai Lake Stone with inscription Dulefeng. At the back of

福字碑　Fu stele

独乐峰　Dule stone

北京胡同文化之旅
A CULTURE TOUR TO
BEIJING HUTONG

the stone, there is a bat-shaped pool and a pile of rockeries. There is a Yaoyue Pavilion on the top with climbing corridors at two sides. Then the Beatitude Palace distinguishes itself by the elegant architecture. In the east yard, there is a great theatre with Goulianda roof. Huxin Pavillion is also called Shuixie. The rockery ship in the west of the garden is the palace for fishing of the owner. Liubei Pavillion in the east of Rockery is special and there is a wide water trough on the flow. And when guests gathered together in the pavillion, the owner put a wine cup an the flowing water in the trough. It's the turn for someone writing poem when the cup stopped by.This is called enjoying Qushui Liu shang. Inside the garden, cypress and flowers can be found everywhere which embodies all features of typical Qing gardens.

湖心亭
Huxin pavilion

园中的最高点"邀月台"
The culmination of the garden: the Yaoyue Platform

花园北侧的"蝠厅"
Hall of bats to the north side of the garden

花园的西洋门　Foreign style gate of the garden

北京胡同文化之旅
A CULTURE TOUR TO BEIJING HUTONG

梅兰芳故居　The Former Residence of Mr. Mei Lanfang

在护国寺大街路北有座幽静的四合院，这就是已故京剧表演艺术家梅兰芳先生的寓所。梅兰芳（1894～1961年），字畹华，江苏泰州人。他继承和发展了京剧旦角行当表演艺术，形成了具有独特风格的"梅派"，名列"四大名旦"之首。他的表演艺术在国内外享有极高的声誉，代表剧目有《宇宙锋》《贵妃醉酒》《西施》《生死恨》《霸王别姬》《穆桂英挂帅》等，拍摄电影片《梅兰芳舞台艺术》《游园惊梦》，成功塑造了赵艳容、杨玉环、虞姬、杜丽娘、穆桂英等艺术形象。梅先生自1950年至逝世前在此院居住。正院里的北屋明间是小客厅，客厅两侧是他的书房"缀玉轩"，东侧是起居室。西厢房辟为"戏曲艺术"资料室，收藏着1965年梅夫人捐献的3万多种珍贵资料，东厢房陈列梅兰芳在国际文化交流活动中的图片和资料。

The tranquil quadrangle in the north road of Huguo Temple Street is the former residence of the great artist Mei Lanfang in Peking Opera. Mei Lanfang (1894 ～ 1961), was born in Taizhou, Jingsu province in 1894. It is he who inherited and developed the Dan character (the female character type in Chinese operas) in Peking Opera and initiated the characteristic Mei Style. He is the top player in the Four Famous Dan Characters and had a great reputation in and abroad. The representatives of his plays are as follows: the Peak

《天女散花》梅兰芳饰天女
Fairy in Fairy Disseminating Flowers acted by Mr. Mei Lanfan

梅兰芳故居近照
Memorial of Mr. Mei Lanfang

梅兰芳故居院内一景
Spot in the former residence of Mr. Mei Lanfang

of the Universe, the Drunken High-ranked Imperial Concubine, Beauty Xishi, Life and Death, the Overlord's Departure and Female General Mu Guiying. He has been shot in the movies, the Art of Mei Lanfang and Dream in Garden. The popular artist images such as Zhao Yanrong, Yang Yuhuan, Yuji, Du Liniang and Mu Guiying are endowed with great vital force. Mr. Mei Lanfang has lived here since 1950 until he passed away. The north room was once used as parlor and his study Jade Room lies next the parlor. The bedroom in the east side while the west side-room is used as an exhibition room for over thirty thousand valuable materials donated by Mrs. Mei in 1965.

火德真君庙 The Temple of the Firefiend

在地安门外大街路西有一座建于元代的火德真君庙，俗称火神庙，是市级文物保护单位。山门内建有钟鼓二楼和四层殿。真君庙是京城保存完好的大型庙宇，更是地安门古桥畔的一景。

The Temple of the Firefiend, built in Yuan Dynasty, locates in the west road of outer Di'an Gate Street which is in the list municipal cultural protection units. There are two Bell towers inside the gate and a four-story palace. The well-kept temple attracts many tourists in and abroad.

广化寺 Guanghua Temple

该寺位于鼓楼西侧鸦儿胡同内，始建于元代，明清时重修过。其山门坐北朝南，庙内钟鼓二楼、天王殿、大雄宝殿及藏经楼等建筑至今完好，并保存有明清石碑和书法刻石数处，现为北京市文物保护单位。

The temple locates in Ya'er Hutong west to the drum tower and was first built in Yuan Dynasty, rebuilt in Ming and Qing Dynasty. The gate sits in the north and facing the south. There are some wellkept buildings in the temple, such as the bell tower and drum tower, Tianwang palace, Daxiong palace and library. There are also some stone steles and calligraphy steles of Ming and Qing Dynasty in the temple.

火德真君庙
The Temple of the Fire-fiend

广化寺
Guanghua Temple

张之洞故居
The Former Residence of Mr. Zhang Zhidong

该宅在白米斜街路西，是清末洋务派首领张之洞故居。院内建有花厅和楼房，前后廊子相连，很有特色。现为西城区文物保护单位。

The house lies in the west road of the Rice diagonal street and it was once the residence for Mr. Zhang Zhidong , the leader of Foreign- separative Wing in late Qing Dynasty. There are parterre and buildings inside the yard, linked by corridors back and forth. It is now in the list of the municipal cultural protection units.

烤肉季　Ji's BBQ Restaurant

位于银锭桥北的烤肉季饭庄有着百余年的历史。在清道光年间，季德彩经营烤羊肉，店名"烤肉季"。季氏烤肉历史悠久，在烤肉的吃法和作料调配上保持传统特色，深受顾客欢迎，是京城有名的老字号。

This BBQ restaurant north to the Yindian Bridge has a over one hundred years' history. During Daoguang Years in Qing Dynasty, Mr. Ji Decai ran the restaurant and gained great popularity for its special cooking flavor and characteristic flovoring.

张之洞故居
The former residence of Mr. Zhang Zhidong

烤肉季　Ji's BBQ restaurant

汇通祠　Huitong Temple

　　在什刹海西端的小岛上有一组古建，清乾隆时曾重修，定名汇通祠。山上有碑亭，乾隆皇帝的两首诗刻在碑上。该祠坐北朝南，山门虽小，但很独特。院内大殿前曾保留形如鸡、狮的奇石一块。后鸡狮石丢失。今天复建汇通祠，郭守敬纪念馆设在院内，是人们观景、休闲的好去处。

　　On the island to the west side of Shi chahai, there are a forest of ancient buildings rebuilt by Emperor Qianlong in Qing Dynasty and named Huitong Temple. There is a pavilion up the hill with two poems written by Emperor Qianlong on the stele. The temple sit in the north and facing the south with a small but special gate. There was once a peculiar stone in shape of a chicken and a lion, but unfortunately, it was lost. Today, the temple is the memorial to Guo Shoujing, a nice spot for residents here for entertainment and sight-seeing.

西海汇通祠（今郭守敬纪念馆）
Huitong Temple in West Sea (Memorial of Mr.Guo Shoujing)

银锭观山一景
Mountain vision from Yinding Bridge

银锭桥
Yindian bridge

银锭观山　Mountain Vision from Yinding Bridge

在烟袋斜街西口，紧连什刹海景区有座小石桥，古称银锭桥。此桥虽小，名气甚大，乃"燕京小八景"之"银锭观山"。每当夕阳到来，在晚霞的辉映下，游人站在桥上远眺西山，美景尽收眼底。

To the west of Yandai Diagonal Street, there is a plain bridge named Yinding Bridge. Although there is no special for the looking, the bridge has a big fame since it is one of the Eight Pictures of Beijing. At the sunset time, people standing on this bridge can overlook the Fragrant Hill which composes an attractive scene.

白大成与他的"盘中戏"
Mr. Bai Dacheng and His Plate Play

京城民间艺术家、鬃人制作大师白大成先生的家就是西城区首家家庭艺术馆。他

白大成先生
Mr. Bai Dacheng

盘中戏传统京剧人物
Characters in traditional Peking Opera

盘中戏"闹天宫"
Stirring up the welkin

所制的北京传统鬃人,以京剧人物为主,放在古老的铜盘中,表演起来,剧中人物活跃转动,甚是精彩,闪烁着中国民间艺术的灵气。

    Mr. Bai Dacheng, the folk culture artist, makes his home the first family museum in the West District. He is good at making the clay figurine whose bottom is affixed with bristle. Then the clay figurine plays the Peking Opera in the ancient bronze plate which endows the characters with life and energy.

三、西城区胡同游（南线）

自前门西大街老舍茶馆往西，淡蓝色车棚上标着"你好北京"字样的三轮车整齐排列，这就是宣武区胡同游的首发站。在导游的带领下，胡同游车队出发了。经过大耳胡同、石猴街、茶儿胡同这些老街巷，车子走走停停，游客可以随导游步行一段路，观赏北京胡同四合院的如意门门楼，精美的门头砖雕"富贵牡丹"、"松鹤延年"等图案，以及门簪上的木雕"迪吉"（其意是我来到吉祥的地方）。也有临街的大门上雕刻着"忠厚传家久诗书继世长"的对联，这显示了宅主人的治家之道。一对石门墩上，雕刻蝙蝠和古钱币的图案，其意是"福在眼前"。听着导游的讲述，游客们对古老的胡同建筑有了较全面的了解。进入四合院，游客会受到居民热忱的接待，这里有红花盛开的石榴树，葡萄架下可与主人一起品茶、聊天。随后车队来到了延寿寺街。老街仅几百米，但有关延寿寺，历史上留下了"坐井观天"的传说。今天这里是商业区，还存留着京城仅有的老邮局。再前行，东、西琉璃厂老街又呈现在眼前。这是京城古老的文化街，古玩、字画、碑帖、文房四宝、印章、古籍书刊商店比比皆是，游客在这里拍照购物，久久不愿离去。宣武区胡同游的终点站是西河沿老街的正乙祠戏楼。在这座有着300余年历史的戏楼舞台上，京剧艺术大师程长庚、杨小楼、梅兰芳都曾登台献艺，在艺术史上留下了光辉的一页。旅游者可以在此观赏京剧，受到艺术熏陶。城南胡同游全程两小时，给中外游客展现出京城宣南文化的历史画卷，让人们流连忘返。宣武区胡同游的另一条路线是，经过灯市街去游览大栅栏步行街。该街长达300余米，有着数百年的历史，是繁华的商业街。这里有始建于清代的同仁堂中药店、马聚源帽店、内联升鞋店等数家京城老店铺，还有老戏院和电影院，是旅游购物的好去处。

Hutong Tour in West District(South Route)

West to the Laoshe Tea House, lines of pedicabs with Hello Beijing on the blue shed are waiting. This is the start of Xuanwu Hutong tour. The parade goes ahead under the lead of the tour guide, passing through the Da'er Hutong, Shihou Street and Cha'er Hutong, and then the tourists can walk with the guide together to enjoy all specials in the Hutong. You can see Ruyi Gate of quadrangle: peony, cypress and crane are carved on the stone, and Diji wood engraving on the head means welcome for all the guests to this lucky place. On the gate, you can see couplets like Honesty and tolerance will pass down son to son, while the Book of Songs and the Four Books will spread generation by generation. On one pair of piers, there are bats and ancient coins carved on it which means an access to happiness. Tourists come to have a better understanding of Hutong culture. Stepping inside the quadrangle, local people give a warm reception to all guests who can chat while drinking tea under the grape and megranate with red flowers. Yanshousi Street is the next stop. Although only several hundred meters long, there is an idiom, having a very narrow view, about it. Now, it is a commercial street and an ancient post office can still be seen in this street. Then we come to the east and west Liulichang Street, the prosperous culture street with curio stores, painting stores, stores for rubbing from a stone inscription, stores for the four treasures of the study, i.e. writing brush, ink stick, ink slab and paper, seal stores and stores for ancient books. Tourists love taking pictures of the ancient street as well as shopping in all unique stores. The termination of this tour is the Zhengyici Theatre in west bank Old Street. The theatre has a history more than three hundred years, on the stage of which masters like Cheng Changgeng, Yang Xiaolou and Mei Lanfang have performed. Tourists can watch the Peking Opera here and experience the traditional cultural elite. Two-hour tour in south Beijing provides a good chance for tourists around the world to understand the culture connotation of south area of Beijing. Passing DengShi street to tour Dazhalan walking street, 300 meters in length is another route. With hundreds of history, Dazhalan Street is a prospering business street, and there are many old shops, such as Tongrentang Drugstore, Majuyuan Hattery, Neilansheng Shoemaker of Qing Dynasty, old theater and cinema.

延寿寺街　Yanshousi Street

　　这是一条清代老街，为繁华的商业区，原有古庙延寿寺。宋代徽、钦二帝被金兵掳至中都（即今北京），关押在这里，留下了"坐井观天"的成语。今寺已废，只留下了街名。

　　This is a prosperous commercial street first built in Qing Dynasty. There was once a Yanshou Temple where Emperors Hui and Qin of Song Dynasty were imprisoned here when they caught by Jin guards. It is also the place the idiom having a very narrow view comes from. The temple has been destroyed now and we can only imagine it from the name of the street.

老邮局　The Old Post Office

　　这是一座有着百余年历史的老邮局，自清末至今建筑保持原样，一直是为居民服务的邮电所。在京城，这样历史悠久的邮局为数极少，因此也成了旅游者关注的景点。

　　This is an old post office with a more than hundred-year history. It was built in the late Qing Dynasty and remained the same as its origin, always working as the post office. There are few such old post offices which make it a spot for tourists.

东琉璃厂街口的老邮局
Old post office in east Liulichang Street

东琉璃厂老街
Old Liulichang Street

琉璃厂文化古街
The Old Culture Street in Liulichang

和平门外的琉璃厂文化街，分为东街和西街，因明代这里曾开设过琉璃窑厂而得此街名。这里历史上有古玩店、字画店、碑帖店……其名气很大。20世纪50年代初，中国书店又建在这里，经营古旧书刊。20世纪80年代这条老街进行了修复和改建，东、西街的交界处，建成一座汉白玉石桥，甚是壮观。现东街上有宝古斋、松筠阁、墨缘阁经营名人字画、印章、碑帖，很有特色。西街有荣宝斋和创建于1904年的庆云堂，后者是一座二层楼的老店，这里开设古代钱币收藏以及金石拓片、文房四宝等收藏。旁边的观复斋的经营也独有特点。在中国书店，还可以购到新印古籍和古旧书刊。今日琉璃街文化古街又焕发了青春。

The Liulichang culture street out of Heping Gate is divided into East Street and West Street. The name Liulichang comes from a Liuli stove here in Ming Dynasty. There have been curio stores, painting stores and stores for rubbing from a stone inscription, which brought it a great fame. In the early fifties of twenty century, the Bookstore of China was settled here to sell the old books. The old street was reconstructed and a white marble bridge was erected at the crossing of the east street and west street. The Baoguzhai, Songyunge and Moyuange are all famous stores for calligraphy, painting, seals and rubbings. The Rongbaozhai and Qingyuntang built in 1904 are in the west road. The later store is a twostoried store where you can find ancient coins, rubbings and the four treasures of the study, i.e. writing brush, ink-stick, ink-slab and paper. The neighbor Guanfuzhai is also a characteristic store. While in the Bookstore of China, reprints of ancient books can be found. The old street has restored to its original prosperity.

西琉璃厂街上的老店铺
Old store in west Liulichang Street

京城老店荣宝斋　Old store Rongbaozhai

东琉璃厂街的老店铺
Curio store in East Liulichang Street

北京胡同文化之旅
A CULTURE TOUR TO
BEIJING HUTONG

西琉璃厂老街（李海川 摄） Old Liulichang street (by Li Haichuan)

东琉璃厂街上的古玩店 Curio store in East Liulichang street

老店萃文阁 Curio store of Cuiwenge

中国书店　The Bookstore of China

　　这是一家老书店，位于东琉璃厂西口路北。其旧址是元代的海王村。至清乾隆时已成书画、碑帖的集市，因比邻火神庙，形成每年正月新春的厂甸庙会。该书店开办于解放初期，历史悠久，专门经营古旧书籍。每逢春节，这里正处庙会的繁华地段，顾客盈门。平时也是来琉璃厂文化街的中外游客光临之地。

The old bookstore lies on the north of East street of Liulichang. The site was Haiwangchun in Yuan Dynasty and became a market of books, paintings and rubbings in Qianlong times, Qing Dynasty. It's because nearby the Firefiend Temple that it came into being a temple fair in New Spring of the first month of Lunar calendar. The long-history bookstore founded sooner after Liberation is an exclusive monopoly store of ancient and old books. when it's the chinese New Year, the customers are crowded here for it lies in the prosperous place. It's a must to the visitors, who come to Liulichang culture street, to visit the bookstore.

状元府　The Mansion of Number One Scholar

　　这是一座三进大四合院，原是清代一位状元的府第。进了广亮大门来至外院，这里南屋曾是书房，里院是长辈和儿孙们居住的地方。历经沧桑变幻，如今这里已是幼

中国书店（李海川 摄）
The Bookstore of China (by Li Haichuan)

店内一角
Corner of the Bookstore of China

清代状元府第
The Mansion of No.1 Scholar in Qing Dynasty

儿园，古老的院落又获得了青春。旅游团队经常到此，了解老北京的生活，并与小朋友合影留念。

This ternary quadrangle is a residence of Number One Scholar in Qing Dynasty. Through the Guangliang Gate, you can see the study at the outer yard and the bedrooms for the owner and his sons in the inner yard. This has turned to be a kinder garden after so many years. The old courtyard seems to shine again with the kids. This is a must for tourists here and they can visit the ancient architecture while taking pictures with kids.

梨园工会　Liyuan Labour Union

清代乾隆年间徽班进京，是我国戏曲史上的昌盛时期。因京剧演员的职业称为"梨园行"，后来就诞生了"梨园行会"。今天位于樱桃斜街路北的这座老四合院，就是历史上的行会旧址，又称为梨园新馆。院内原设有议事厅和办公室等。现该院广亮大门的门簪上还存有"梨园永固"四个字。

It's the high time for the theater history of China that the Hui opera group came to Beijing in Qianlong time, Qing Dynasty. Actors of Opera was called Liyuan Profession, soon the Liyuan Theatre Guild came to being. The old quadrangle lying in the north of Yingtao Inclined Street is the site of the guild and it got another name of Liyuan New Yard. There are meeting room and office in the yard and the words of Liyuan Forever can be seen on the clasps of the Guangliang gate.

王瑶卿故居　The Former Residence of Wang Yaoqing

在大栅栏西口往南的培英胡同里有个老四合院，这是已故著名京剧旦角艺术大师王瑶卿先生的住所。王瑶卿的"王派"，是京剧旦角艺术的基本流派，在京剧史上有过巨大的贡献。新中国成立以后，他担任中国戏曲实验学校校长，为培养年青一代京剧表演艺术工作者，作了始终不懈的努力。在唱的方面，他对京剧传统规律有所突破和创新，尤其在

梨园工会旧址
Former residence of Liyuan Labour Union

王瑶卿故居大门楼（李海川 摄）
The front gate of the former residence of Wang Yaoqing (by Li Haichuan)

主人的正房
Main room of the house-owner

中国京剧院的《柳荫记》剧中，他在音乐和唱腔设计的尝试上取得了成功，受到了观众的喜爱和好评。

There is an old quadrangle inside the Peiying Hutong south to the Dazhalan which is the former residence of Wang Yaoqing. Wang Style is a fundamental genre in Dan character of Peking Opera and it has contributed a lot to the history of Peking Opera. After the founding of PRC, he worked as the principal of Chinese Opera Experimental School and did his best in helping and educating a young generation of Peking Opera. He also did a lot of improvement and creation in singing of the traditional opera. His Liuyin Legend is one successful example in music and singing style which has gained great popularity and fame.

王瑶卿在京剧《四郎探母》中扮演铁镜公主
Wang Yaoqing acted as the Princess of Iron Mirror in the opera the 4th Son Visiting His Mother

廊房头条老店铺　The Old Store in Langfang 1st Lane

在清代至民国年间，大栅栏往北的廊房头条老街上开有珠宝店、首饰楼、玉器、制印、锦盒等店铺。经营很有特色。今开，还可以见到这些老店的部分建筑。这座西洋式的商店，原是座金店，现门面上还有"金店"二字，是原址遗存。

北京胡同文化之旅
A CULTURE TOUR TO BEIJING HUTONG

廊房头条老金店旧地全景
Parvorama of the old jewellery store in Langfang 1st Lane

There're many jewellery shop, headgear plaza and various shops, such as jade articles, making-seal and suitcase in the old street of Langfang 1st Lane on the north of Dazhalan Street. Now some buildings are well kept. The occidentalism shop in the picture was a gold shop and we can read the words of JIN DIAN.

黔之会馆 Qianzhi Assembly Hall

位于樱桃斜街11号的长宫饭店，昔日是京城的黔之会馆。始建于乾隆年间，至今已200余年历史。中式木楼典雅别致，格调古朴，气势恢宏，建筑独特，这里天井庭院、廊檐缭绕，双层相映。清代科考届期，士子习居。民国时蔡锷将军曾住这里，产生与小凤仙的一段佳话。新中国建立后，叶剑英元帅来此视察，精辟指点，使此楼得以保存。现在老会馆变成了旅社，多次被电视剧组借用，拍摄了多部故事片，也成了胡同游的一个景观，引来了众多的中外游客。

The Changgong Hotel, No. 11 in Yingtao Diagonal Street, is the former Qianzhi Assembly Hall which was first built in Qianlong times, Qing Dynasty and has had a history of over two hundred years. The architecture is a wooden tower, althoughsimple and unsophisticated, it has a larruping style with majestic vigor. The building has a dooryard, together with the modillion, forming a binary vision in the courtyard. Examines all over the country lived here when they got the chance to attend the national test in Qing Dynasty. In the times of the Republic of China, General Cai'e has lived here for a period and there is a beautiful story about him and Xiaofengxian. After the PRC. founded, general Ye inspected here which helped to preserve this hall until now. Today, the hall has come to be a hotel. It has been rent by many film studios and it is also a scenic spot in Hutong tour which is attractive to tourists around the world.

古老的黔之会馆一角
Corner of Qianzhi Assembly Hall

正乙祠戏楼门前
Gate of zhengyici Theatre

正乙祠戏楼举办演唱会
Performance in the theatre of Zhengyici

正乙祠戏楼　Zhengyici Theatre

位于西河沿老街路南的正乙祠戏楼有着 300 余年历史。它是全木结构的古建筑，分两层，楼下能容 200 余名观众，楼上设包厢。京剧艺术大师程长庚、杨小楼、梅兰芳都曾在此登台献艺。

The theatre, over three-hundred-year old, locates in the south road of the old street by the west bank. It is a two-storied wooden architecture which can hold two hundred audiences downstairs at one time. Private balconies are on the second floor. Celebrities like Cheng Changgeng, Yang Xiaolou and Mei Lanfang have all been on this stage once.

裘盛戎故居
The Former Residence of Qiu Shengrong

在正乙祠戏楼大门的对面，有一座四合院，这就是已故著名京剧表演艺术家裘盛戎先生的寓所。裘盛戎（1915～1971 年）出身梨园世家，其父是名净裘桂仙，自幼随父学艺，又在富连成社坐科，出科以后，在和金少山、杨小楼诸名家的长期合作中，吸取了花脸各家和其他行当的长处，对花脸的声腔、板式进行了突破，达到声情并茂、以韵味取胜，形成了观众喜爱的"裘派"。新中国成立后在北京京剧团任副团长，代表剧目有《将相和》《赤桑镇》《赵氏孤儿》《林则徐》《杜鹃山》等。

裘盛戎故居
The former residence of Qiu Shengrong

大栅栏街瑞蚨祥
Ruifuxiang Silk Store in Dazhalan Street

On the opposite of the theatre of Zhengyi ancestral temple, there is a quadrangle which is the former residence of Qiu Shengrong, a famous departed artist in Peking Opera. Mr. Qiu Shengrong (1915-1971) was born in a well-known opera family, the father of whom is Mr. Qiu Guixian, a famed Jing (character with painted facial make-up in Peking Opera). Mr. Qiu Shengrong learned from his father when he was very young and then he spent several years in Fuliancheng. He has been cooperated with Jin Shaoshan and Yang Xiaolou, from the experience of which he summarized and improved the sound and form of Hualian and consequently, he created the popular Qiu genre in opera. After the liberation, he worked as the vice president of Beijing Peking Opera troupe. His representatives are as follows: the Harmony of the General and the Minister, Righteousness Above Family Loyalty, the Orphan of Zhao Family, Lin Zexu and Cuckoo Hill.

瑞蚨祥绸布店　Ruifuxiang Silk Store

该店位于大栅栏街路北，是专营绸缎、布匹的百年老店。它以货真价实、礼貌待客闻名全城。"十年动乱"期间，瑞蚨祥的匾额被摘掉，改名"荣昌号"。改革开放以后，"瑞蚨祥绸布店"的老牌匾又挂出来，货品更为丰富，每日迎接着大量国内外的顾客。

Standing at the north road of Dazhalan Commercial Street, the Ruifuxiang Silk Store, which is almost one hundred years old, is an exclusive store for silk and cloth. It is famous since it's through and courteous all the time. During the Cultural Revolution, the tablet with Ruifuxiang was taken away and the store was renamed Rongchanghao. After the Open and Reform, Ruifuxiang Silk Store get its tablet back and welcome customers throughout the world with more abundant merchandise.

大栅栏步行街　The Walking Street in Dazhalan

大栅栏古街位于前门大街路西。它处在繁华的闹市区，东起前门大街，西至煤市街，全长 300 余米，曾有"繁华市井何处有，大栅栏内去转游"的佳句。此街至今已有 500 余年的历史。这里有始建于清康熙八年的老药铺同仁堂，经营丸、散、膏、丹等成药，闻名中外；还有开业于清嘉庆十六年的马聚源帽店，早年为皇室和贵族制帽；开业于清咸丰三年的内联升鞋店，这里生产的千层底布鞋深受顾客欢迎。瑞蚨祥绸布店、张一元茶庄等，经营的商品也各具特色。早年这里还有"庆乐戏院"和"大观楼电影院"等娱乐场所。新中国成立后，老街进行了整顿和改建，又增加了百货商场和妇女儿童服装店等。建为步行街后，引来了众多顾客和中外旅游者。

West to the Qianmen Street, Dazhalan is three hundred meters long, east from the Qianmen Street and west to the Meishi Street. It is said that, where to find a prosperous and busy fair? Dazhalan has all what you want. More than five hundred years old, the street has many old stores. Tongrentang Drugstore opened in the eighth year of Kangxi, Qing Dynasty, which is famous for patent medicines including pilular, ointment and pellets. Majuyuan Hattery, once the inclusive hattery for royal families and nobles, was open in the 16th year of Jiaqing times, Qing Dynasty. Neiliansheng Shoemaker was open in the 3rd year of Xianfeng times, Qing Dynasty, which is famous for fabric shoes. There are many other old stores such as Ruifuxiang Silk Store and Zhangyiyuan Tea House. There had been Qingle Theatre and Daguanlou Cinema in the street. After the founding of the People's Republic of China, the street was reconstructed into a walking street and department stores and stores for women and children are open here. It has become a must for tourists around the world.

同仁堂药店　Tongrentang Drugstore

同仁堂老店铺距今已有300年的历史，创建于清康熙四十一年。因由乐姓人家经营，百姓们称其为"乐家老药铺"。该店曾为清皇室制御药，声誉大振，是国药行业中历史最悠久、信誉最佳、驰名中外的名店。

The first Tongrentang Drugstore was founded in the 41st year of Kangxi times, Qing Dynasty, who has an over three-hundredyear history. The family name of the owner of the drugstore is Le, so people called it Le drugstore. It gained its fame for making medicine for the royal family. Tongrentang Drugstore is a worldfamous store who has the oldest history and best reputation.

广德楼剧场　Guangdelou Theatre

该戏楼建于清末，早年京剧界的名家都曾在此登台献艺。20世纪50年代改名为前门小剧场，专门演出北京曲艺。因其处于大栅栏街路北的繁华地段，吸引了众多的观众。90年代该楼进行了重建，又恢复了广德楼的名字，现由北京市曲艺团在这里演出曲艺和相声。

The theatre was built in late Qing Dynasty and was the spotlight years before where many celebrities have been on the stage. It was renamed Qianmen Little The-atre fifty years ago and then became an exclusive theatre for Beijing Dramatic Balladry. It was still a popular place because of its advantageous location in the north road of the prosperous Dazhalan Street. The theatre was reconstructed in nineties of twenty century and got its former name Guangdelou Theatre back. Today, it is a fixed spot of dramatic balladry and comic dialogue performance for Beijing Dramatic Balladry Society.

同仁堂药店　Tongrentang Drugstore

大栅栏街广德楼
The gate of Guangdelou theatre in Dazhalan Street

六必居　The Liubiju Pickles Store

位于大栅栏东口粮食店街的六必居酱园，始建于明嘉靖年间。这里产的酱菜香甜味美，且经济实惠，至今已有400余年历史。六必居酱菜已成为旅京客人携带赠送亲朋的佳品。

Lying in the Liangshidian street, at the east of Dazhalan, and the Liubiju Pickles Store was first built in Jiajing times Ming Dynasty. The pickles here are cheap but delicious which has a good fame for over four hundred years. The pickles here come to be a nice present for friends and relatives.

前门清真寺　The Mosque in Front Gate

该寺位于扬威胡同，始建于明初，至今已有500余年的历史，建筑风格独具。清康熙、乾隆时重修，现尚有山门和一座勾连搭屋顶的礼拜殿。院内还保存着阿拉伯文碑，是区文物保护单位。

北京胡同文化之旅
A CULTURE TOUR TO BEIJING HUTONG

六必居老店　The old pickles store Liubiju

六必居店内一角
Corner of the pickles store Liubiju

大栅栏地区的古老清真寺
The old Mosque in Dazhalan Street

This mosque lies in the Yangwei Hutong and it has a history of over five hundred years since it was built in Ming Dynasty. The mosque has been twice reconstructed in Kangxi and Qianlong times, Qing Dynasty. Today, an outer gate and a bethel with Goulianda style roof can still be seen. Besides, there is a tablet with Arabian inscription in the courtyard. The mosque is district cultural relic's preservation site.

杨小楼故居　The Former Residence of Yang Xiaolou

京剧武生泰斗杨小楼先生，在清光绪三十二年被选入升平署进宫承差，后与梅兰芳共组崇林社。杨先生的拿手剧目有《安天会》《状元印》《霸王别姬》等。笤帚胡同39号院北屋三间为杨先生所住，自1914年至1938年的24个春秋，他生活、说戏、练功都在这里。今该院保存完好。

The Wuda mater in Peking Opera, Mr. Yang Xiaolou, was selected to the Shengping Office of the Forbidden City in the 32nd year of Guangxu times, Qing Dynasty. He, together with Mr. Mei Lanfang, established the Chonglin School. The adept operas of Mr. Yang include Antian Meeting, the Marking of the First Scholar and All-conquering King Parts with His Favorite Concubine. The three north rooms of No.39 in Saozhou Hutong are the residence of Mr. Yang. He lived here, practiced here and made rehearsals here from 1914 to 1938 which accounts for twenty-four years. The courtyard is still well-kept today.

纪晓岚故居 The Former Residence of Ji Xiaolan

虎坊桥路口往东、珠市口西大街241号是清乾隆年间主编《四库全书》的纪晓岚先生的故居。现院里保存着"阅微草堂"，是主人的书房。前院的古藤萝、后院的海棠树为纪先生亲手所植。今天，故居已整饬一新，对外开放。

京剧名家杨小楼故居
Former residence of Peking Opera Celebrity, Yang Xiaolou

纪晓岚故居一景
Former residence of Ji Xiaolan

京剧名家杨小楼演出的剧照
Photo of famed Opera actor Yang Xiaolou on show

北京胡同文化之旅
A CULTURE TOUR TO
BEIJING HUTONG

纪晓岚故居的古藤
Old vine in former residence of Ji Xiaolan

East to the Hufangqiao Road, No. 241 West Street of Zhushikou, is the former resience of Ji Xiaolan, who edited the Imperial Collection of Four in Qianlong times,Qing Dynasty. The famous Yueweicaotang, the study of Mr. Ji is well-kept in the courtyard. The cirrus in the front yard and the Chinese flowering crabapple in the back yard were planted by Mr. Ji himself. After a complete decoration, the residence has been opened to tourists.

湖广会馆　Huguang Assembly Hall

广安大街路南的湖广会馆有着悠久的历史，这里有座木制古戏楼，清代梨园名家均在此献艺。民国时孙中山先生北上，曾在这里的舞台上进行过几次演讲。院内还有一座古井，名为"子午井"，相传每天中午12时至1时，该井的水非常甜。今天，湖广会馆已成为北京戏曲博物馆。每晚这座古戏楼都安排京剧演出，深受中外旅游者的欢迎。

湖广会馆正门（李思 摄）
The front gate of Huguang Assembly Hall (by Li Si)

Huguang Assembly Hall lies in the south road of Guang'an Street. Many celebrities of Liyuan in Qing Dynasty have performed in the wooden theatre inside the assembly hall. During the Republic of China, Sun Yat-sen has made several speeches on this stage. The well inside the yard is called Ziwu well, the water of which turns out to be extremely sweet from twelve o'clock to one o'clock at noon. Now, it is the opera museum of Beijing and there are performances of Peking Opera every night here, which is popular among tourists.

一品香浴池　Yipinxiang Bathhouse

湖广会馆戏楼内景
Huguang Assembly Hall

大栅栏地区有多条斜街，其中王广福斜街名声很大，此街现名"棕树斜街"。从前街的两头有个表演曲艺大鼓的场子，中间有个百年老澡堂，名为"一品香"，在大栅栏地区很有名。

局部
Details

浴池遗址（李海川 摄）
Relics of the Yipinxiang Bath House (by Li Haichuan)

今天该浴池遗址尚存建筑完好。

There are some diagonal street in Dazhalan district, and one of the famous street was Guangfu diagonal street which is now named Zonglushu Diagonal street. Once upon a time a theatre for tom-tom was on one of side of the street and an old famous bathhouse Yipinxiang was in the middle. Now the bathhouse is well kept.

三井胡同　Sanjing Hutong

大栅栏地区的三井胡同，因有一眼水井而得名。刻井的石板盖上有三个大小等同的圆孔为"品"字形，百姓称其为三眼井。

The Sanjing Hutong in Dazhalan area is famous for the water well. There are three coordinative round holes which look like Chinese character Pin on the well cover, and that is why it is named so.

北京胡同文化之旅
A CULTURE TOUR TO BEIJING HUTONG

真武庙近照（李海川 摄）
A close look at Zhenwu Temple
(by Li Haichuan)

游人在老街拍照（王超 摄）
Tourists are taking photos in the old street
(by Wangchao)

真武庙　Zhenwu Temple

该庙始建于明代，位于该地区路北的小巷里。其庙门坐东朝西，院内主殿尚存，可谓是京城仅存的一座真武庙了。

Zhenwu Temple was constructed in Ming Dynasty and it locates inside a narrow lane in this area. The gate of the temple sits in the east, facing the west. We can still see the main hall of the temple which might be the only Zhenwu Temple in Beijing.

门框胡同　Menkuang Hutong

这是大栅栏街路北的一条小胡同，在北头还保存有青石所砌的门框，人们习惯称其为门框胡同。巷子里卖北京小吃的店铺居多，著名的爆肚冯经济、年糕王就在这里，还有卖豆汁、烧饼、豆腐脑、豌豆黄、茶汤等京味小吃的店铺。在此用餐经济实惠，历来吸引了众多的顾客。

Menkuang Hutong is a narrow Hutong in the north road in Dazhalan area. The bluestone doorframe is still well-kept and then it is called the Menkuang Hutong (Doorframe Hutong). There are many fast-food stores inside the Hutong especially for the traditional Beijing snacks such as Feng's pig tripe store and Wang's rice cake store. Besides, snacks like bean juice, baked cake, bean curd soup, pea cake and tea soup are also available in this unnoted lane. Many tourists are attracted by their taste and boon.

走进百姓家
Stepping into the House of Local People

为了让国外旅游者深入了解四合院里居民生活，导游可以带客人来到百姓家，观赏花木、鱼虫、叙家常、学学包饺子，吃顿家常饭，与居民一起合影留念。

In order to let the foreign tourists have a better understanding of local people's life, the tour guide will lead the tourists into house of local people. They can enjoy the traditional plants, chat with local guys, and learn to make dumplings, have dinner with the locals or take pictures together.

外宾在百姓家留影（陆军 摄）
Foreign guests taking pictures with folks (by Lu Jun)

外宾在学包饺子
Foreign guests learning to make dumplings

附 / 老北京胡同民情风俗画

Appendix / Genre Painting of Beijing Hutong

何大齐 绘

by He Daqi

老北京民风民俗多姿多彩，三教九流各呈特色。何大齐先生所绘的老北京胡同民情风俗图，展现了当年市井下层人民的生活风貌。新中国建立后，随着社会的发展，过去的一些行当或萎缩，或演变，或绝迹，但我们从文学作品和影视戏剧中，还能窥见其风貌。重温这些画面，既可以让我们体会到时代的变迁、生活的提高，也可以丰富我们的历史知识，加深对社会生活的认识。

Beijing has a rich folk customs and traditions while these Beijing Hutong Folk Panorama by He Daqi, show part of the life and living condition of the lowlife in the old time. After the founding of PRC, with the development of the society, many oldtimey activities has faded or changed even vanished which we can only review through the literary works or movies and so on. This picture really reminds us of the vicissitude of the society, the improvement of our living condition. Meanwhile, it gives us a chance to enrich our historic knowledge as well as to have a better understanding of our society.

附　老北京胡同民情风俗画
Appendix　Genre Painting of Beijing Hutong

拜年图　Happy Chinese New Year

打鼓的　Playing drum

卖空竹图　Selling Kongzhu

送水图　Delivering water

北京胡同文化之旅
A CULTURE TOUR TO BEIJING HUTONG

街头小贩　Peddle on the street

卖小金鱼　Selling little goldfish

捏江米人图　Piaching Jiangmi person

夏日乘凉图　Cooling in summer

附　老北京胡同民情风俗画
Appendix　Genre Painting of Beijing Hutong

卖胡琴图　Selling Huqin

结婚花轿　Litter for marriage

剃头挑子图　Facility of haircut

耍猴栗子图　Playing monkeys with chestnut

159

北京胡同文化之旅
A CULTURE TOUR TO BEIJING HUTONG

卖噗噗噔　Sellig Pupudeng

磨剪子磨刀图　Grinding knives and scissors

锔盆锔碗图　Patching pot, bowl and basin

算命图　Fortune-telling

附　老北京胡同民情风俗画
Appendix　Genre Painting of Beijing Hutong

摇煤球图
Rocking coalball

窝脖儿 Wobo'er

拉洋片图　Showing diorama

耍猴图
Playing monkeys

附 北京的流杯亭
Appendix　Pavilions of Floating Cups in Beijing

　　我国古建筑多多姿彩，"流杯亭"就是具有独特风格的建筑。这种亭子除具有一般古建筑的特征外，就是亭内地面的汉白玉石雕有弯弯曲曲的水槽，宽10厘米左右、深15厘米，引清凉泉水流过，细心静听是一种享受。

　　古老的北京现存流杯亭四处。最古老的一处流杯亭在京西九十里的潭柘寺内。该寺据清《潭柘山岫云寺志》记述：寺建于晋代，本名嘉福寺。距今已有一千七百年的历史。当地老百姓都称该庙为潭柘寺，故有"先有潭柘寺，后有北京城"的说法。寺内有一亭，名为"猗轩亭"，匾额为清乾隆皇帝御书。亭内地面是一块巨大汉白玉石基，石上刻有蟠龙似的水槽。从北边看水道如虎头，从南边看又像龙尾。相传古代每年三月三日文人在此欢聚饮酒，将酒杯放在石槽内随水飘流。酒杯停在谁的身边，就罚酒一盅，或即兴吟诗一首。据文献所记，清康熙、乾隆皇帝曾数次来此游玩，现在亭北面还有乾隆皇帝住过的寝室及宝座。

　　京城内中南海瀛台流杯亭，俗称流水音。该亭中的水道流水时似有乐声，很是美妙。皇帝同他的辅臣常在此饮酒对诗。吟诗时要将斟满的酒杯放入水槽龙头处，然后随水飘动。当酒杯被流水推至水槽末端时，诗就得吟出。由皇帝先吟，大臣们随后和诗。在乾隆皇帝《御制诗集》中赞此亭云："凭栏俯碧流，佳景喜相酬。素色因心静，清音与耳谋。仙人捧醇酎，春鸟弄箜篌。恶旨思前戎，盈科悟进修。"

　　故宫里的乾隆花园，建在假山旁的禊赏亭是一处更为精巧的流杯亭。它设计得独具匠心，该亭的水源来自假山上专筑的大缸，经人工安排流水入亭内。此外，位于北城的恭王府花园里有座流杯亭，名"沁秋亭"。亭内所刻水槽与前面不同。曲折回旋为"亭"字形，其槽雕刻很有气势。该亭旁边有井，需人工取水倒入亭内水道，以达"曲水流觞"之乐。这些昔日王公赏乐的流杯亭，今天已成为中外游人观赏的景点。

　　另外，在位于香山公园内的香山饭店庭院（美籍华裔建筑师贝聿铭先生设计），建筑师们精心设计了一座新型的流杯亭。该亭汲取古代建筑特色，并结合现代科技，以水泵引水上山，后急流而下，造成水幕的效果；然后顷水道流水入亭，恰似亭中涌泉。这是园林建筑中的佳作。

总之，京城的数座流杯亭，将以其独有的特色，为北京的旅游景点增添风采。

The architecture styles in China are colorful. The Pavilion of Floating Cups in Beijing is a representative in the field of traditional ancient architecture. The most special point about it is a meandering canal made of white marble under the pavilion, which is about 10cm wide, 15cm deep. The clear spring water is running slowly in the meandering canal.

There are four Pavilions of Floating Cups preserved well in Beijing today. They are the national key cultural relics protection units. The Pavilion of Floating Cup with the longest history in Tanzhe Temple called Yixuan Pavilion lies in the west of Beijing. According to the records, Youyun Temple on Tanzhe Mountain, Tanze Temple was built in Jin Dynasty, 1700 years ago. So there is a vivid saying that it is built before Beijing city. The Emperor Qianlong inscribed on a horizontal inscribed board for it. The most famous point is the meandering canal made of white marble which is like a drag shad under the pavilion. It is said that many scholar in ancient times drunk in the pavilion on the third day of March of the lunar calendar in Beijing. They put a cup on the spring water in the canal，seeing a cup floating. He must be made to drink as a forfeit or wrote a poem when the cup stopped facing on someone. According to the records, Emperor Kangxi and Emperor Qianlong had ever been in here for sightseeing and enjoyment several times.

There is another pavilion of floating cups named the Sound of Flowing Water in Zhongnanhai. The sound of flowing water in a meandering canal likes some nice soothing music. Emperors and his ministers often drank and rhymed here.

The third one to be introduced is named Xishang Pavilion built near a rockery in the Emperor's Qianlong garden of the Forbidden City which has been open to the public in recent years. The source of water in the canal under the pavilion is from the water vat on the rockery. The fourth Pavilion of Floating Cups lies in the Prince Gong's Palace Garden in the Northern Beijing city named Pinqiu Pavilion. The shade of the canal under the pavilion is a Chinese character '亭', the distinguishing feature. The source of water is from a well nearby.

流杯亭之一　The First of the pavilions of Floating-cups

流杯亭之二　The Second of the pavilions of Floating-cups

Besides those given above, a new pavilion of floating cups was designed by world famous architect I. M. Pei in the Beijing Fragrant Hill Hotel built in 1982.The water in the canal under the pavilion is from feed water pumps system, so the manual techniques about it make the water in the canal. Its beautiful sight remains in every visitor's and forever.

In a word, these several pavilions of floating cups have been the representative sights in Beijing.

附 北京 33 片历史文化保护区
Appendix　The 33 Places under Historical and Cultural Protection in Beijing

　　在城市历史建筑保护方面，20世纪90年代初北京市做出了两项重大决定，一是加快危旧房的改造，改善京城百姓的居住条件，二是公布了第一批历史文化保护区。第一批确定南长街、北长街、西华门大街、南池子、北池子、东华门大街、文津街、景山前街、景山东街、景山西街、陟山门街、景山后街、地安门大街、五四大街、什刹海地区、南锣鼓巷、国子监地区、阜成门内大街、西四北一条至八条、东四北三条至八条、东交民巷、大栅栏地区、东琉璃厂、鲜鱼口地区共计25片，之后又陆续公布了第二批、第三批，包括皇城、北锣鼓巷、张自忠路南、张自忠路北、法源寺以及新太仓、东四南、南闹市口等，三批共计33片。在这些保护区内，有众多的景点和文物古迹。

　　登上景山的万春亭，古老的故宫尽在眼底。当你漫步在那正南正北，东西交错，恰似棋盘的胡同地区，结构独特的四合院门楼呈现在眼前，这是北京人代代生活在这里的天人合一的布局，大、中、小型的四合院建筑是世界大都市中的奇观，这就是北京的胡同。在这些保护地区，都有其悠久的历史和文物景观。东城区的南锣鼓巷是条南北长巷，东西有对称的十六条胡同，建成于元代，历经明清数百年的风云变化，至今依然保持原样。有些胡同的名称，如雨儿胡同、板厂胡同、沙井胡同……至今还沿用着元代的名字。其南北主街与对称的胡同组成了蜈蚣形，老百姓称之为"蜈蚣巷"。胡同里不同类型的四合院建筑甚是完整，广亮大门、如意门处处可见。这里保存着清代总督府、皇亲宅第、行辕和名人故居，市级文物保护单位"可园"也在这里。一些古老宅院门楼前还保存着清代的上下马石以及雕刻精美的门头砖雕，刻有花卉图案或文字的门簪。大门左右还配有一对石雕的抱鼓石或门枕石，人们俗称之为门墩儿。其造型独特，上面雕有小石狮，多数被砸掉了头尾，这是百年以上的活化石，都有着它自己的故事。门楼前的古槐树是四合院历史的见证。浏览南锣鼓巷地区，不仅可以欣赏、考证四合院建筑，还可以了解胡同文化及民俗。西城区的西四北一条至八条地区，至今保持着明清两代的格局，四合院保存完整。北头条原名驴肉胡同，北二条清代为帅府胡同，北三条名报子胡同，至1965年才改称北儿条。这些胡同里保存着清代四合院多处，还保留着完整的门楼、照壁和垂花门。有的院落里两侧是抄手游廊，墙上建有什锦灯窗及精美的砖雕图案。北三条胡同还有一座带花园的四合院，院内爬山游廊及太湖石相映生辉，真可谓清代四合院的典范。该地区还有名人故居，著名京剧表演艺术家、"四大名旦"之一的程砚秋先生故居即在这条胡同里。这些地区还有多处文物保护单位，以上仅举两片地区为例。今天，这些保护地区历史风貌犹存，各具特色。

读者如有空暇，浏览这些历史文化保护区，置身于胡同古韵中，既可开阔眼界，又可以对老胡同进行研究考证，增添对胡同文化及民俗的了解。

The first block of historical and cultural site under protection in Beijing two decision on old city area was made by Beijing government in the beginning of 1990s: One is to accelerate the reconstruction of dangerous-worn building to improve the living condition of Beijing citizens. The another is proclamation of the first block of historical and cultural site under protection including 25 places: the South Long Street, the North Long Street, Xihuamen Street, Nanchizi, Beichizi, Donghuamen Street, Wenjin Street, Jingshan Front Street, Jingshan East Street, Zhishanmen Street, Jingshan Back Street, Di'anmen Street, Wusi Street, Shishahai District, Nanluoguxiang, Guozijian District, Fuchengmen Inner Street, Xisi Street(from North 1-8 Alley),Dongsi Street(from North 3-8 Alley), Dongjiaominxiang, Dashilan, Liulichang East Street, Xianyuhou,etc. After that, the Second and third block of historical and cultural site includes Imperial city, Beiluogu Xiang, the south & North of Zhangzizhong Rood, Fayuan Temple, New Taicang, South of Dongsi, South of Naoshikou. Among those protection area, there are many scenic spots culture relics.

Mounting on the Wanchun Pavilion, one can enjoy the ancient Imperial palace in the birds eye. Wondering among the chessboard-constructed areas consisting of alleys from east to west or from the east to west, you can spot uniquely-designed quadrangle gates. Those large, medium and small scaled quadrangle construction, which accommodate the Beijing people for generations, constructed the layout of great harmony between people and heaven-alley. Those preserve areas boasted time-honored historical and culture scenic Nanluogu Xiang, which located in the Dongcheng district, is a long alley from north to south. Taking Nanluogu Xiang as axis, 16 symmetrical alley was arranged along it. Despite hundreds years of weathering and changeable situations throughout the Ming and Qing dynasties, those alleys still remains their original appearances. Some of them, such as Yu'er Hutong, Banchang Hutong, Shajing Hutong, still keep the name originated from Yuan dynasty. The south-north oriented main street and the 16 symmetrical east-west oriented alleys present the shape of Wugong(centipede, a kind of reptile), hence popularly known as the Centipede Alleys. The alley boast rows of neat quadrangles with gates of varied styles, such as Guangling Gates and Ruyi Gates. The mansion of viceroy in Qing dynasty, the residence of the imperial relationships, thrill and former residence of celebrities are preserved here. Ke Yuan, the protect unit of Beijing city, is located here as well. Some age-old dwellings still preserve Qing dynasty stepping stones for mounting or dismounting from a horse in front of their gates, gate heads carved with exquisite patterns and gate claps decorated with wood carvings of flowers and words. On both sides of the gates there are well-sculptured round drum stones or rectangular gate pillows. The stone lions carved on the uniquely-designed stones, most of which are damaged with head or tails cut, all have stories behind them. The old locust trees in front of the gates are the long history witness of quadrangle. While visiting the alley area around Nanluogu Xiang, tourists can not only appreciate and research the quadrangle construction there but also get some understanding of the folk customs and culture in alleys. In the western part of the city, the time-honored alley area from the First alley to the Eighth Alley still retains the original layout of the Ming and Qing dynasties with quadrangles well preserved. As far as the alley are concerned, it was not until 1965 that their original names in the Ming and Qing dynasties were changed to the North Xth(1st, 2nd, 3rd,...) Alley. For example, the North First Alley, the North Second Alley and the North Third Alley were originally named Lurou (Donkey Meat) Alley, Shuaifu Alley and Baozi Alley respectively (Shuaifu was the official residence of a commander in chief, and Baozi refers to an official announcement of a candidates success in the imperial examinations or of an officials promotion in ancient China). The alleys here boast many well-preserved quadrangle of Qing dynasty, gates, screen walls and doors with flower-dangled. After entering some of the quadrangle, you can find a dropping flowers gate, on each side of the gate there is a short-cut corridor with a row of open windows of different styles bearing a variety of elegant brick carving on the wall. Many dwellings have been rated as historical and cultural site under protection, here listed are two examples: No.39 in the alley is the former residence of Cheng Yanqiu, a famous artist of Beijing opera performance and one of the four masters playing female roles in Beijing opera. In the Third Alley, a classical 3-layer-court-yard quadrangle with a garden, bearing a splendid combination of a winding veranda and Taihu rocks(boulders found on the edge of Lake Tai), may be rated as a model of quadrangles of the Qing dynasty. Today, 33 historical and cultural site under protection retains their historical appearance with respective characteristics.

On a vacation, you should visit those historical and cultural site under protection in order to widen your knowledge, do research on ancient alleys, get more under-standing on the culture, folk customs of alleys and enjoying yourself in the rhythms of ancient alleys.

图书在版编目(CIP)数据

北京胡同文化之旅/李明德编著. —北京：中国城市出版社，2019.5
ISBN 978-7-5074-3189-6

Ⅰ.①北… Ⅱ.①李… Ⅲ.①胡同-介绍-北京-汉、英 Ⅳ.①K921

中国版本图书馆CIP数据核字（2019）第077772号

责任编辑：张幼平
责任校对：赵昕雨

北京胡同文化之旅
A CULTURE TOUR TO BEIJING HUTONG

李明德　编著
WRITTEN BY LI MINGDE

*

中国城市出版社出版、发行（北京海淀三里河路9号）
各地新华书店、建筑书店经销
北京方舟正佳图文设计有限公司制版
天津图文方嘉印刷有限公司印刷

*

开本：889×1194毫米　1/20　印张：8⅗　字数：142千字
2019年10月第一版　2019年10月第一次印刷
定价：68.00元
ISBN 978-7-5074-3189-6
　　　（904155）

版权所有　翻印必究
如有印装质量问题，可寄本社退换
（邮政编码 100037）